R.I.S.E.

Responsibility Increases Self-Esteem

Featuring Special Program Supports:
- Character Education
- Anti-Bullying
- Social Skills Curriculum
- R.I.S.E. @ Home

Roger A. Fazzone, Ed.D.

Eighth Edition 2013

outskirtspress
DENVER, COLORADO

Outskirts Press, Inc.
http://www.outskirtspress.com

ISBN: 978-1-4787-0110-1

Outskirts Press and the "OP" logo are trademarks belonging to Outskirts Press, Inc.

PRINTED IN THE UNITED STATES OF AMERICA

Acknowledgements

I wish to express my personal and professional gratitude to the Shelby Cullom Davis Foundation for their generous support. The vision and encouragement of Diana Spencer are especially appreciated.

Many individuals are involved in the evolution of any complex learning system, most notably the faculty and staff who administer the daily implementation of the R.I.S.E. Program. Their willingness to embrace concepts and techniques contributed greatly to this sixth edition.

Over the years, I have come to rely upon the critical comments and proofreading assistance of Donna Konkolics. Her suggestions have been invaluable. The social skills course outlines and the appendix were written by Jennifer Scully – a true medievalist.

The sixth edition features historical material and updated forms and procedures of the Responsibility Increases Self-Esteem (R.I.S.E.) Program. Eva Rossman was instrumental in developing the history, while Karen Gamble was key in updating the forms used. Their contributions are greatly appreciated.

Contents

Foreword

60 Years: 1945-2005
Educating Minds and Building Character
By Eva Rossman

During the 1930's, the sleepy hamlet of Amenia was home to a unique religious retreat named Secret. The School was founded by Coral "Sunny" Barlow, a Christian Scientist (CS) practitioner living in New York City, her husband Bill Barlow and her brother Rex Armin.

The 1930's witnessed the infamous Lindbergh kidnapping, and many wealthy families were concerned about the safety of their children. In the years following the Lindbergh events, Sunny was encouraged, by some of her wealthier clients, to provide a retreat to learn/study/work on Christian Science principles. In response to these urgings, she bought a farm in Amenia/Northeast, New York, which she transformed into a private, secluded boarding school, originally named Secret and later renamed Viewpoint. Two of her clients, Mrs. Worral Hyde and Mrs. George W. Merck, supported her efforts and became substantial benefactors.

Some of the children who attended Viewpoint possessed physical and/or cognitive disabilities. Sunny accepted these youngsters into her school with the hope of helping them through her Christian Scientist faith. One of the youngsters with a handicapping condition was John "Johnny" Merck, son of George and Serena Merck from New Jersey. Mrs. Merck was a devout woman who enrolled all three of her children in Viewpoint School.

In 1943, Marge Heckel came to stay at Viewpoint with her friend and counselor, Sunny Barlow. Marge had just lost her husband due to illness. Still recovering from her loss, and in order to renew her faith, she decided to spend some time at Viewpoint with Sunny. Marge had worked as a dental hygienist, although she had no formal degrees or training. In order to occupy Marge during her stay at Viewpoint, Sunny asked Marge to work with the handicapped students, caring for them and imparting whatever knowledge possible.

During the summer of 1943, Barbara Finger enrolled in Viewpoint. At that time, Barbara was going through a difficult period because her mother was quite ill and not expected to live much longer. Her father thought it best for her to live under the care and guidance of Sunny Barlow. She recalls, "Viewpoint provided me with a caring world and a fantastic education." Since it was a very small private school and Barbara was the only student taking the advanced Math and Latin classes, for all practical purposes she was being tutored in those subjects. According to Barbara, in addition to a quality scholastic curriculum, Viewpoint offered tennis, horseback riding, and speech lessons.

Looking back on her experiences from a 2002 perspective, Barbara hesitates to describe Viewpoint as a "Prep" school, for it also became a safe place for several disabled students for whom other placements were not available in those days. This led to a student body comprised of a few disabled students, along with a larger group very qualified to attend college. She recalls the senior class of 1942 consisted of Serena "Bambi" Merck, Hester Pinchon, and Frances Lake, among others.

Sunny's Christian Scientist practice also served the purpose of recruiting students to Viewpoint. As word of her works became more widely dispersed, the student body became more diverse. In 1943 Chang Nai Kim, or "Chum" as he was called, was the lone male in the graduating class. Chum's family was part of a group of intellectuals who had fled Korea during the tumultuous times of the Second World War and Japanese occupation. Later his two sisters came to Amenia, and lived with their mother in a nearby farmhouse also owned by Sunny. Barbara was in the class of 1947 along with Joyce White, Joan Dean, and Sally Funk.

As Viewpoint increased the size of the student body, there was some pressure placed on the school to become "accredited" by New York State. Also, when prospective families visited the school to explore possible enrollment of their child, some were taken aback by the presence of handicapped students. This created a second pressure point for Sunny to deal with – ending the care and teaching of the handicapped students.

During this time, Marge had become an excellent caregiver and educator to these students, and would take them for a ride in the country whenever prospective students were visiting the school. Although an effective way to deal with one of Sunny's "pressures," this was merely a temporary solution. Marge grew to enjoy working with these youngsters and became an advocate for them. She felt that they could be happy and have a productive life living on a farm, and doing the simple tasks required for independence.

Serena Merck was delighted with Viewpoint and felt Johnny was in the "right" place under the care of Marge and with the prayers and support of Sunny. Her two daughters, Judith and

Serena, were also enrolled at Viewpoint. Both were very active and prospered under Sunny's careful eye. Julian Strauss, an Amenia youngster, lived just down the street from Viewpoint and as a day student attended the lower grades. He remembers the young Serena, who had acquired the name Bambi from her grandmother, as the prettiest girl in the school and a polite, very bright friend. The girls rather enjoyed the boarding school life, while their parents felt they were safe and in the capable hands of a very moral woman.

The autumn of 1944 was noteworthy for several reasons including the baseball world, which was treated to an all St. Louis World Series. The mighty Cardinals, with Stan "The Man" Musial, were being challenged by the lowly Browns, their cross-town rivals featuring Pete Gray, a one-armed right fielder. As the year moved to a close, these three women decided to start a boarding school for youngsters who learn differently and might also possess physical handicaps. Sunny Barlow would provide the educational guidance, Marge Finger would provide the nurturing care, and Serena Merck would provide the bulk of the finances necessary for such a venture. As the year 1945 started, the women searched for an ideal location for their very special school. They probably didn't realize it at the time, but their school would be only the second boarding school for students with learning disabilities in New York State. The first was the Gow School located near Buffalo, New York, which was founded in 1925 and served students with dyslexia. The Thompson Farm, owned by Ed Thompson was primarily a chicken farm. Since the economics for farmers were poor in the Hudson Valley during the war years, Ed Thompson decided to sell 12 acres of his land located on the west side of Route 22 in Amenia. There was a farmhouse and several barns on the property.

When Sunny Barlow found out the land and buildings were for sale she must have been uncontrollably excited, and after discussing it with Marge they informed Mrs. Merck. It was perfect: the farmhouse would be both the dining hall and the residence hall for all, and the barns could be converted into classroom space. It was also located close to Viewpoint, so Sunny could oversee everything. Best of all, the children would be safe and receive proper schooling in etiquette, practical skills, and reading, writing, and arithmetic.

The three founders were surely excited over the prospect of starting a program for the handicapped students living at Viewpoint. They consulted with each other, as well as some parents with children with handicapping conditions, and from these conversations, they determined what needed to be done to convert the large farmhouse and other structures. Sunny hired some local carpenters to do the work and she and Marge made sure all was being done according to plan. John Finger was one of the local men working on this project. He was married with a teenage daughter and a very sick wife, and really became involved with the restoration project. John's wife passed away peacefully in 1944 and his daughter, Barbara, became deeply involved in Viewpoint. She, as a student, and he, as a craftsman, were preparing for the opening of a new and exciting school.

They both became very friendly with Marge, who could empathize with John since she had recently lost her husband. She also took an immediate liking to Barbara, who became very distraught when her mother was nearing the end. All three were sure that God would help them through their time of sorrow and near despair. As work progressed on readying Maplebrook Farm for the arrival of the first eight students in September 1945, the three founders agreed on the basic philosophy and curriculum of the school. The new school would emphasize good manners, faith in God, basic self-help skills, and practical academics. Marge would be the Director of the school, while Sunny would be available for support and guidance at her campus two miles up the road. Eight students moved to the new campus and took up residence among eleven employees, including Marge Heckel and John Finger. The first bi-weekly payroll was issued in 1945 and totaled $287.50.

Marjorie Heckel, although the Director of Maplebrook Farm, chose to be known as "Aunt Marge" by the Maplebrook Community, and was the virtual heart and soul of the school. She brought more than just "book learning" to the daily life of the students. In providing a home away from home, her school became a challenging family environment. In this cozy atmosphere, teachers and staff sat interspersed with students in the dining hall at mealtime (a practice that continues today almost sixty-five years later). Sunny would visit Marge on Sundays and there would be singing and readings from the Good Book*. One Sunday per month, Marge would have the girls serve tea to Sunny and the others with all the proper etiquette observed. The "tradition" of no elbows on the table started with Sunny at Viewpoint and was brought to Maplebrook by Aunt Marge.

The emphasis on work and manners were other "carryovers" from Viewpoint. Maplebrook students received extensive training in achieving the social graces. Weekly classes included "Posture and Charm," speech and conversation, ballroom dancing, and a Saturday evening social followed by refreshments in the Girls' House.

Science and Health, by Mary Baker Eddy.

Part I
The Program

1

Introduction

Since its founding in 1945, Maplebrook has sought to provide quality programs addressing the needs of children said to be slow learners, or who may exhibit learning disorders.

The setting in historic Dutchess County, one mile north of the village of Amenia, New York, is ideal for such an undertaking. It is remote, yet it affords many opportunities for youngsters to interact with the outside world in a non-threatening environment, and to gain confidence in their abilities.

Maplebrook's academic program has been specifically designed to challenge students in the acquisition of basic educational skills. Students are encouraged, through a combination of remedial and compensatory learning techniques, to apply traditional academic courses in a variety of structured settings focused on preparation for independent living.

The living environment at Maplebrook is conceived to stimulate the development of social skills that will enable youngsters to participate in the greater community. Dormitory life emulates family life, with students taking responsibility for maintaining a homelike atmosphere. Sit-down meals are in the dining room. Students develop acceptable table manners by observing those at the table and clearing when the meal is finished.

Maplebrook provides a year-round sports program capitalizing on excellent on-campus facilities as well as the spectacular terrain of Dutchess County. A pool, gymnasium, tennis courts, and ample playing fields are supplemented by neighboring lakes, mountains, and trails.

The entire Maplebrook experience is constructed to allow youngsters maximum exposure to postsecondary studies. The Center for the Advancement of Postsecondary Studies was established to allow youngsters the opportunity to pursue guided study toward developing career skills or, in some cases, the pursuit of college degrees. For those choosing career education, half of their week will be spent "on the job" in the community. These settings are places where they learn skills in retailing, office routine and equipment, day care, elder care, construction trades, horticulture, food service, culinary arts and print shop. The skills in these areas are quite intense, and the student earns a certificate of studies upon completion of the curriculum. Other students may earn certificates in computer skills or nursing assistant through our partnerships with local postsecondary institutions. Finally, some youngsters who are deemed able to profit from a collegiate setting attend Dutchess Community College in nearby Poughkeepsie. They are monitored and tutored by an experienced Maplebrook teacher who coordinates the program. All students are taught Life Centered Career Education (LCCE) skills according to the curriculum established by Deschler from the University of Kansas.

Underlying the entire Maplebrook experience is a consistent effort to instill values that will enable youngsters to make appropriate choices and enjoy life to its fullest.

The mission of Maplebrook School is to provide quality academic programs for youngsters with learning differences and/or who may exhibit a learning disorder. Through small-group and individualized instruction, the student will be assisted in reaching his/her academic, social, vocational and physical potential. In addition, the caring, supportive and homelike environment provides the necessary experiences to allow youngsters the opportunity to assume a more independent role in society.

More specifically, the goals of Maplebrook are to:

1. Provide an academic curriculum designed to enhance strengths and remediate academic weaknesses.

2. Provide an environment where the student develops self-awareness and social skills to participate appropriately.

3. Provide a setting where the student develops a peer support system consisting of companionship, friendship and support.

4. Offer a wide variety of structured and non-structured physical activities designed to assist the student in the areas of health care, physical fitness and sportsmanship.

5. Offer career education in occupational and vocational fields designed to provide job training for immediate or future entry into additional career training and/or employment.

6. Provide life-skills education to assist the student in the acquisition of independent living skills.

7. Facilitate the acquisition and understanding of universally accepted moral principles.

8. Provide direction to parents to assist them in planning future educational opportunities for their children.

A key ingredient in the recipe of success with learning-handicapped students is the correct mixture of concerned and dedicated faculty and meaningful programs. Fortunately, the traditions of Maplebrook School are well established and demand excellence.

The Culture of the School

The existence of Maplebrook School stems from its mission, which is to educate students with learning differences. The core of our mission is to help students grow academically, socially and ethically. Keys to student success are the structure and support provided through Maplebrook's programs, faculty and staff, and a caring, welcoming environment.

The faculty has designed programs to challenge the students in academics, expand their experience in athletics, support their acquisition of social skills, and facilitate the integration of universally accepted values. Using teaching tools, the RISE (Responsibility Increases Self-Esteem) Program, and a compassionate attitude, students are encouraged to internalize lessons both in and out of the classroom and grow to be morally good people. The constituencies within the School promote opportunities for our students that challenge and strengthen healthy self-esteem, and develop good character.

Since its founding in 1945, Maplebrook School has created a safe, structured, family-like atmosphere for faculty, staff and students. The traditions established by Marge Finger, founding Head of School, were reinforced by Lon Adams, second Head of School, expanded by Roger Fazzone, and are continued today by Donna Konkolics, our fourth Head of School. These traditions have been carefully cultivated, and are the foundation of the culture of Maplebrook School. Courses, academic requirements, the physical plant, staff and students have changed as the School has progressed, but the basic tenets of promoting quality academics, character development, social skills and independence remain the same. The School makes every effort to further educate everyone involved with Maplebrook in the history of the School, as well as the principles on which it was founded.

The School's leaders – the Board of Trustees, Senior Teachers, Master Teachers, Department Heads and Administrators – endorse the School's mission statement and make decisions consistent with the School's philosophy. Parents of students enrolled, as well as parents of alumni, believe in the mission of Maplebrook School, and support not only growth of students, but also growth of the School as a whole.

The School continues to educate students, staff, parents and alumni about the mission and goals to help with a complete understanding. There is an abundance of support for our programs, however, not everyone is aware of how these programs contribute to the culture of the School. Maplebrook School encourages families to become more active in the education of their children, with a particular focus on those parents who live at a distance from the School. The mission and goals are emphasized during the orientation of new faculty and staff, as well as being incorporated more frequently within professional staff development programs.

Central to the success of Maplebrook is the education of students who can profit from our programs. The School's admission process has been developed and advanced to include recommendations from the faculty. Care is taken so that persons from different areas of the School have input as to the ability of a student to benefit from all aspects of the School.

Maplebrook School's boarding school structure is the key to its ability to carry out the mission of the School. Long hours are devoted to the quality education we provide to our students, as well as the atmosphere created by the founders and still carried out today. A dedicated staff willingly chooses to share their lives and learn along with the students. The School has done much to make dormitory life more comfortable, and continues to explore an improved quality of life for faculty who live in the dormitories if there is room for such improvement. Programs have been developed to help faculty who do not reside in the dormitories understand all aspects of boarding school life.

All in all, Maplebrook School has a clearly defined mission: a mission governed by both the mind and the heart. Those involved with the School believe in the intellectual and moral growth of our students, as well as the growth of the entire school. We foster independence and success through our programs, and especially through the School's character education initiatives. The School has found many ways to better integrate all programs centered on moral development.

2

Self-Esteem

Frequently, youngsters who experience difficulty in learning develop a chronic problem of poor self concept. A child's concept of himself is forged slowly over time. The sum total of life experiences and interactions with a variety of individuals create this perception of self. Geiser (1973) indicates, "One's concept of self can be broken down into many interrelated parts... feelings of self-worth, feelings of competence, and a sense of self-identity." All of our interactions with our students help reinforce their existing view of themselves. In fact, it is this central reality that provides an opportunity to shape an environment where the student develops self-awareness and social skills to participate appropriately in the community.

A precise definition of what we mean when we speak of self-esteem is crucial to understanding the scope of the problem. In education and psychology, exact definitions are at times elusive. For instance, there are several existing explanations of the meaning of learning disabilities currently in practice, although little agreement on what precisely constitutes the disorder. The literature review conducted by the University of California

(1989) was studied and modified by the California Task Force to Promote Self-Esteem and Personal and Social Responsibility to state that self-esteem is "...appreciating my own worth and importance and having the character to be accountable for myself and to act responsibly toward others." This definition possesses far-reaching consequences for all individuals in society. The implication is that a direct link exists between a healthy self-esteem and socially responsible behavior.

Assuming the importance of self-esteem on affecting behavior, it would be prudent to understand the possible influences on self-esteem. William James (1890) indicated our achievements in this world are measured against our aspirations in any given area of behavior. If achievement approaches or meets aspirations in a valued area, the result is high self-esteem. Coopersmith (1967) summarized, "James concludes that achievement is measured against aspiration with valued areas assuming particular significance, but he also believes that men achieve a sense of success and status." Therefore, there are at least two major determinants of self-esteem. First, what one thinks of himself, and, second, what one thinks others think of him. Most theorists on the subject of self-esteem recognize the influence of these two factors in the formation of one's view of self.

Our students are impacted by these same forces – what they think of themselves and what they think others think of them. Therefore, each interaction a student has at Maplebrook School influences his view of self – each success, each failure, each correction, each word of encouragement. When a student is able to master his environment, he comes to view himself in a positive manner. Unfortunately, the converse is also true in that a student who feels unable to master his environment feels inadequate and regards himself poorly. It is our task to structure an environment that fosters a healthy growth in the self-esteem of each Maplebrook student. In the publication, *Towards a State of Self-Esteem* (1990), the following possibilities for the field of education are espoused:

In the twenty-first century, self-esteem and personal and social responsibility are integral parts of a lifelong process. Schools welcome and support children, regardless of sex, race, nationality, creed, or socio-economic status. Students are seen as precious and deserving of recognition and attention.

Schools provide rich educational experiences that are designed to:

- Awaken the learner in each student.

- Develop each child's learning capacity and appreciation for learning as a lifelong experience.

- Provide an education that appreciates the uniqueness of each child.

- Address the special needs of every student.

- Serve to liberate rather than domesticate.

- Promote responsible character and values.

- Provide children with role models, experiences and skills necessary to develop their own creativity, intuition, and imagination.

Schools are operated by administrators and teachers who have experienced self-esteem education, who esteem themselves, and who are valued by their communities and by the systems they work for. They are sensitive to and comfortable with students of all races and learning styles, they know how to teach students to esteem themselves, they are positive role models.

These are magnificent possibilities and may help us create lofty goals for ourselves and our students. We must keep in mind that we are unable to give an individual high self-esteem, but we are able to create an environment that facilitates the opportunities for students to feel better about themselves. When we accept the principle that all individuals, including ourselves, deserve to be treated with dignity and respect, we create an environment based on mutuality.

3

The Environment

Knowledgeable practitioners in the field of residential education voice strong support for the concept of therapeutic milieu and its positive potential for students. The environment consists of the total experience of everyday living – the other children, the staff, the programming and the physical setting. Unfortunately, although much has been written about the milieu as a potential therapeutic tool, little systematic knowledge has been acquired regarding its development. Redl (1966) reflected, "I should like to find out, not only what milieu is and how it operates, but also how we can describe it, how we can influence it, and by what actions of all involved is it, in turn, created and molded. At the moment I am convinced of only one thing for sure – we all have quite a way to go to achieve either of these tasks."

As we study the impact of the environment on students in a residential setting, it becomes apparent that a key ingredient is the interaction with professional staff members. Trieschman (1969) has attempted "to present a loose phenomenology of the milieu as a teaching tool. What goes on daily between children and adults is seen as an opportunity for therapeutic education or re-education of the child. The practitioners of the art of child care are our primary audience. They are the main teachers in a child-rearing milieu." These individuals are, of course, the employees of the School – everyone who interacts with the student. The single most important impact on a student lies within the quality of his daily interactions and relationships. Therefore, an understanding of the basic elements of establishing and maintaining relationships is crucial to the success of creating an environment where growth and development are possible.

4

Relationships

Every educator invests a great deal of his workday in the presence of children. The majority of the children he deals with are in need of positive growth experiences to help in the development of their ability to deal with the environment in which they live. Few people would deny the important influence an educator may have on the growth and development of children in his care. Considerable attention must be given to the skills necessary to develop the relationships between educator and student if our schools are going to develop children who can function adequately in society.

The Art of Relating

In the field of education, so much has been said and so little has been written on the subject of how an educator can go about establishing relationships. Although it is widely recognized that relationships are of primary importance to successful work with children, little is done to provide workers with a practical basis for developing this skill. Indeed, "skill" may be too powerful a word for a series of behaviors that may, in truth, be relegated to the realm of art. Novice educators are advised to "be yourself, the kids will get to know you," or "start firm with them and once you establish a relationship you can lighten up." Although both suggestions may contain elements of truth, they neglect to describe the actions an educator must perform in order to increase the probability of establishing and developing relationships with students.

As the major adult figure for many of the students in school, the educator must be able to relate to a variety of individuals besides the child. Prior to attempting to define the precise meaning of relationship, it is necessary to clarify the meaning of establishing and developing a set of behaviors which facilitate meaningful and mutual interactions.

Establishing Relationships

The establishment of a relationship with a student or other individual in a school is simply a successful attempt to channel one's behavior toward the goal of starting up a mutual interactive process. The remainder of this section will center upon the behaviors helpful in the "starting up" process with children. It should be noted that most of these behaviors will be successful in dealing with adults as well. Some behaviors crucial to this "starting up" phase are:

1. *Spending time with students.* In education work this is a "given" because it is the nature of the work to be with the students. Spending time, both physically and psychologically, increases the opportunities to share meaningful experiences and thus is crucial.

2. *Allowing students to give and share.* The truism that giving is better than receiving is relevant here. Oftentimes students ask for tangible items and intangible items.

3. *Doing things with students.* Often, because of the role of authority, the adult organizes activities but does not partake in them. It would be beneficial to organize events in which you can be a part.

4. *Caring about students.* Caring is not merely the expression of feelings for the plight of the students. It also means that you will attempt to guide each student in learning to deal with everyday events. A teacher exhibits care for the student by being prepared for work each day and by working in conjunction with the School team to provide the best possible environment. Care is much more than an emotion. It is a purposeful, goal-directed action.

5. *Developing respect for students.* It is difficult for any staff member to have the same type of relationship with every student in the class. Obviously you grow to like some more than others. However, respect is a necessary quality which should be extended to each student. Respect is being aware that the student is a human being with thoughts and emotions, and interacting with him accordingly.

6. *Feeling comfortable with students.* Feeling comfortable does not mean that the worker will become so at ease that he will lose track of his objectivity. But developing a feeling of comfort when in the presence of the student does mean that you are not "on edge" in the relationship.

7. *Developing a sense of give and take.* This is similar to item two, in that a relationship is not one-sided. A relationship works both ways. In a relationship you both give and receive. The educator must maintain his role of authority but there exists a great deal of leeway within those bounds.

8. *Maintaining a realistic perspective of the student's situation.* The educator must understand that while he is obliged to assume some parenting functions, he is not the student's parent. He must maintain a realistic perspective of the student's life situation in that many matters are outside the direct control and influence of the educator. This reality may be one of the most frustrating aspects of education, but will assist in the establishment of a relationship with the student.

Developing Relationships

The obvious task that follows the starting of relationships is working to develop their growth. This development phase also serves the purpose of maintaining the relationship once established. If the educator conceptualized the development phase as similar to an investment of himself to the students – that is, as a commitment to the students in his care – he would understand the immensity of the task at hand. In the field of residential education, the educator is asked to invest or commit himself to the student in his care. The remainder of this section will deal with the behaviors considered helpful in working to develop the growth of relationship. It should once again be noted that most of these behaviors will be considered helpful in working to develop the growth of relationships, and will be successful in dealing with adults as well as children.

Some of the behaviors crucial to this development phase are:

1. *Letting the student know that you like them.* It is always a reinforcing experience to receive compliments or praise. Too often we invest most of our energies in attending to misbehaviors. This tendency can be reversed by praise and compliments for a student's strong points.

2. *Talking with students about the feelings and emotions you experience as a result of events which take place in the group.* We should be careful to maintain a balance of both positive and negative feelings. Too many positive feelings may give students the impression that you are not sincere, while too many negative feelings may "turn them off."

3. *Listening in an active way to what students are saying.* The importance of active listening cannot be overestimated. Active listening, which requires training in Rogerian reflection, is a demonstrable method of interest. We must attend to both the spoken word and the underlying emotion when utilizing this technique.

4. *Understanding the point of view of students.* The educator, in attempting to see the student's point of view, reduces the probability of arbitrary or capricious decision making. This reinforces the student's concept of your respect for his dignity and strengthens the bond of relationships.

5. *Maintaining a personal diary or log to assess the progress of*

relationship development. In many ways, we are similar to a psychotherapist in his interactions with children. Rogers (1967), in reviewing the research of hundreds of studies involving counselors and psychotherapists, found the effective counselor possessed certain characteristics. These characteristics were termed empathy, non-possessive warmth and genuineness. By maintaining a personal log or diary, a professional can review the progress of his relationship development and examine his interactions with students in terms of warmth, empathy and genuineness.

6. *Recognizing the message you transmit to students.* In our everyday interactions with students, we send many messages both knowingly and unknowingly. These messages are transmitted to students through verbal and non-verbal behaviors. These messages become the basis for the development of relationships and much attention must be given to their impact on each student.

Defining Relationship

Prior to this, we have examined some of the behaviors an educator must display in attempting to establish and develop relationships with children. These are practical suggestions, drawn from a theoretical base, which lead to the formation of a helping interaction between an educator and a student. But there can be other types of interactions which lead to a variety of relationships. It is the purpose of this section to explore the basic elements of relationships.

Every relationship contains two essential elements –

attraction and acceptance. Both elements are qualitative labels which refer to a series of behaviors resulting in a set of conditions between individuals. Attraction is the degree to which one individual is drawn to a second individual. Attractions can be positive, negative or neutral. Positive attraction exists when one individual is strongly drawn to a second individual. We state, "Gee, I really like being with Jonathan," when we possess a positive attraction to a particular child. Negative attraction exists when one individual is strongly driven away from a second individual. We describe this situation when we say, "I hate working with José, he makes me wish I called in sick." A neutral attraction is evident when one individual is neither drawn to nor driven from a second individual. The various degrees of attraction and acceptance that are present in any interaction between two individuals determines the type of relationship existing between them.

An interaction which is characterized by a positive attraction and a positive acceptance is called a full psychological relationship. Although this is the ideal for each educator to strive for, it is difficult to reach this high degree of involvement with each student in your class. A marginal relationship is one in which there exists either a neutral or negative attraction with a neutral or positive acceptance. Also, a marginal relationship can occur when there is a neutral or negative acceptance. Many of our relationships are of this variety, and need a great deal of nurturing in order to develop into full psychological relationships. Finally, any interaction which contains both a negative attraction and a negative acceptance is a non-relationship. But for our purposes, we may refer to this as a rebellious relationship, because it might contain the seeds for a more productive relationship.

The Helping Relationship

From what has been discussed thus far, it appears obvious that the goal in establishing relationships with students is, for the educator, to increase the attraction he has towards students, and at the same time display the behaviors which may increase the degree of acceptance students may have toward him. Brendtro (1969) suggests several ways to increase adult attractiveness and minimize adult aversiveness. Among these suggestions is the thought that children who are helped by adults tend to perceive that adult in a more positive manner. It is this helping relationship which facilitates positive ego growth and self-control.

Generally speaking, the goal of helping is to generate more appropriate behaviors. The adult and the child join together to establish these behavioral goals. Then the educator must create the conditions necessary for change to occur. He must control his own behavior and create an atmosphere of trust and security. In essence, he must work toward establishing a full psychological relationship with the student. Once this is approximated, the helping phase may begin.

In order for the educator to help any student, he must become aware of the student's problem. This initial stage of the helping relationship is usually the most difficult because those in positions of authority (teachers) generally assume they know the child's problem. They become judgmental and fail to establish the joining (mutuality) necessary for a true helping relationship. During this initial phase, the educator should facilitate self-exploration on the part of the student, allowing him the opportunity to control as much as possible, the tempo of enunciating the nature of his problem. Once this is accomplished, the teacher should encourage the student to look at the problem from many different vantage points, so that he may better understand the exact nature of the problem. Finally, the student should be assisted in the formation of a plan of action which must be followed in order to resolve this problem.

This scenario may appear to be unrealistic or too complex for the average problem exhibited by students with learning difficulties. It may seem, at first glance, much easier to utilize authority or threats of punishment to have a student alter his behavior. If the goal is merely to control the student, then this technique is not appropriate. But, if the goal includes the concept of teaching the student to control himself, then this technique is essential. It should be recognized that children who are helped to develop self-control do not need adults present to control them. This would surely lighten the burden of most educators and parents.

Responding In a Helping Relationship

Everyday responses are not always appropriate in a helping relationship. An individual who desires to master his role in such a relationship must have a high level of self-awareness and some experience in the "art" of responding. The following is a list of suggestions for professionals who desire to improve their skills in this area.

1. *The educator should concentrate on both the verbal and nonverbal behavior of the student.* This will enable one to obtain more information without the use of questions. Questions remind children of authoritarian relationships and if possible should be avoided in a helping relationship.

2. *If questions must be used, avoid the presence of the pronoun*

"you" in the question. The use of "you" is ego threatening and may reduce the feelings of trust and security necessary for the sharing of information.

3. *The educator should reply to both the subject content and the feelings of the child's message.* Information without feelings is a concept that is acceptable in a court of law, but not in a helping relationship.

4. *The educator should respond in a non-evaluative manner and encourage the student to express himself freely.* Once all the information is available, evaluation responses may be more appropriate.

5. *The educator should avoid "joking" the student out of feeling bad.* This demonstrates a lack of respect for the student's right to feel sad. It would be best to "be there" and understand rather than to interfere. This is most difficult for adults to accomplish because it is uncomfortable to see a child experiencing sadness.

6. *The educator should be aware of his body when speaking with the student.* He should maintain good eye contact while adopting an open posture (avoid crossing legs or arms). Remember that one's body is always communicating.

These suggestions are not meant to be rigid rules which must never be violated. Rather, they are intended as approximate guidelines for facilitating the growth of relationships between student and teacher.

5

Ego Development

Self-esteem is an integral part of the ego development of each individual. As we know, ego is that aspect of one's personality that interacts with one's environment. Each task that must be mastered during a lifetime presents an opportunity for enhancing the development of ego strength, while each task that is failed presents the unfortunate opportunity for weakening the development of ego strength. Therefore, if we, as educators, are skilled in providing adequate ego supports for students, we increase the probability of steady ego development and increased self-esteem.

Trieschman (1969) indicates, "one important aspect of ego development is the capacity to deal with feelings. The ability to cope and use anger, frustration, sadness, longing, excitement, joy, and hope as meaningful parts of human equipment is often missing in our children." These represent various ego tasks which must be strengthened. In a learning environment, youngsters with academic problems will experience considerably more stress on ego functioning than youngsters who have a history of successful learning. Students with learning problems need additional support in order to master the task and demonstrate positive growth.

Ego Supports

Educators have the opportunity to control a major portion of their teaching environment. In a boarding school, the teaching opportunities are extended for the full week and well beyond the formal classroom. Each task of daily living and each interaction with students is a learning opportunity. In order to support students during these potential periods of stress, it is important to develop and maintain good helping relationships. Once these relationships are formed, the crucial task of supporting the student must be addressed. Experience has demonstrated that the following ego support techniques have been successful with youngsters with learning disorders:

1. *Shared Ego* – This is the process of using the educator's strength and stability in helping a student learn an appropriate behavior. In essence, the educator is sharing his strength and support to help a student through a difficult period. Typically, this method would incorporate phrases like, "We can work together to solve this problem" or "I have helped many students who have had this problem, so let's face it together." A derivation of this approach is to utilize the perceived ego strength of a fellow student to assist in crisis. This provides support from a peer to help the student during a time of need. When using this method, phrases such as, "Tracy has been a proctor in this dorm for several months. We may be able to have her help you deal with this problem" or "Recently I helped Tim solve a

similar problem. Let's sit down with him and develop some possible solutions to your problem." Shared ego approaches are often quite comfortable for a student in crisis if the requisite helping relationship has been firmly established. The key ingredient is that a sense of understanding and confidence be conveyed to the student. Our strength and expertise is to act as a temporary crutch to assist students to arrive at solutions to their current difficulties.

2. *External Ego* – Tradition has a great impact on many individuals. In schools, traditions are developed over the years to provide structure and support for students. The rules, regulations, schedules and social structures at any established school can provide this support for all students. Phrases such as, "We expect all students to study hard at Maplebrook," or "At Maplebrook, we behave in an appropriate manner," are frequently used. This technique has the added benefit of correcting an inappropriate behavior without using the pronoun "you" which can be quite threatening to a student with a weak functioning ego system. The concept of the School's tradition giving strength to a student in need of help can be quite comforting. Again, the essential helping relationship is a requisite condition for employing this method.

3. *Ego Components* – Students with learning deficits seem to develop various skills in an uneven manner. For instance, academic success in all but one subject area is not an unusual occurrence. The same pattern can be found in the way in which students have mastered various tasks of everyday life. A student may do well in one area (e.g.

academics) but poorly in another (e.g. group participation). It can be quite helpful to students to help them overcome their deficit areas by building upon their component strengths. For instance, if a student is good at math but has great difficulty participating in team sports, appointing him scorekeeper may be the initial step towards his participation. The underlying idea is to use the student's strength to help address a weakness. Another example may involve a student with good auditory skills who is having difficulty in history because of reading deficiencies. If the student is exposed to a multi-modality approach, the reading deficiencies may be circumvented, and this will increase the probability of successful learning. If we, as educators, utilize a student's component ego strengths to remediate deficit areas, we will advance the growth of self-esteem.

4. *Group Ego* – The vast majority of youngsters are extremely sensitive to the opinions and perceptions of others. In fact, during the teenage years, there is no motivator more powerful than positive peer acceptance. Many of our students have repeatedly experienced failure and subsequent rejection (or perceived rejection) by their peers. A powerful tool for an educator can be support that emanates from a cohesive group. Therefore, it behooves all educators to cultivate a group spirit in their classroom or dormitory, a spirit that exudes pride and mutual respect, a spirit that is not unlike the necessary helping relationship mentioned earlier. When this spirit exists, the group becomes a source of strength to assist students to successfully overcome obstacles in academic and social learning.

6

Teaching Techniques

Each year, thousands of parents and teachers seek professional advice on how to deal with children who exhibit less than appropriate behaviors. The question arises as to how can a well meaning and caring parent or teacher interact with a child who makes their time together unbearable. Perhaps the children are actually teaching parents and teachers to act in odd ways. For example, why would otherwise pleasant, well educated adults find themselves screaming and shouting when dealing with certain youngsters. Further, why would intelligent individuals continue to apply punishment when it appears to have no effect on certain behaviors. The answer to both questions is rather simple – they have not been trained to utilize successful teaching techniques.

Thus far we have explored and recognized the importance of self-esteem on influencing behaviors. We have also detailed the importance that relationships play in the interactions between teacher and student. Building upon these relationships, we have seen how ego support techniques can facilitate the interruption of non-productive behavior. Now what remains is reviewing the methods that can best facilitate the learning of productive behavior. It should be noted that from the multitudinous volumes written on learning theory, four basic techniques have been selected. Experience has proven these basic methods to be quite successful with students who possess learning difficulties.

1. *Insight Learning* – This method requires the recognition of cognitive processes that facilitate the acquisition of knowledge. Assuming the existence of a good helping relationship, students frequently profit from discussions leading to the understanding of why they feel and perform in a certain way. Although the discussion may not lead to immediate results, frequently the student will make a connection and arrive at an understanding of the situation later in life. I would like to illustrate this complex process by describing an experience I had as a youngster. As an eight-year-old growing up in an urban environment, one of my fondest activities was playing stickball. My family lived in a two-story house with a small, treed backyard. Being one of the few grass and treed areas in the neighborhood, our relatives arrived each Sunday afternoon for a day of relaxation and fun that culminated in an elaborate cookout. Part of the Sunday ritual was the division of individuals. The children would flock to the street to play stickball, the mothers would busy themselves with conversation and preparation at the picnic table, and the fathers would retire to a shaded area near the fireplace to discuss local issues and engage in games of chance. One Sunday afternoon, I left the stickball game and returned to the picnic area to get a drink of water. As I approached the area where the water was kept, I observed my father was taking "dead aim" at a squirrel high in a tree. My father was armed with a hand-crafted slingshot loaded with a shiny marble. He launched his deadly missile with great accuracy, and the squirrel fell to the

ground. I was absolutely devastated in observing my father kill this harmless creature. In tears, I chastised him for his cruelty. He looked at me, shaking his head in disagreement, and calmly explained that he couldn't kill the squirrel because he was using a round marble. His logic proceeded to explain that when a round marble hit the round head of the furry creature, it merely stunned him and he would soon recover. He had me help him gather some stones, place them in a circle behind the fireplace, and then he gently placed the unconscious animal in the center of the circle. He told me that if I waited for a few hours, the squirrel would recover and return to the trees. I was relieved, and after a short period of time returned to the stickball game. Several hours passed and the children were called in to supper. I ran to the circle of stones, and sure enough, the squirrel was gone. He had recovered just as my father had indicated.

Ten years later, I sat in my Army barracks in Texas recovering from a brief illness. I was rather lonely, having just turned eighteen and being two thousand miles from home. Then all of a sudden it struck me – my father had fooled me! The round marble, the circle of stone, the explanation, had been an elaborate scheme to reduce the grief of an eight-year-old. But somehow through an unknown cognitive process, ten years later an insight into the incident was gained.

At Maplebrook, the mentoring program allows teachers and students to discuss items of importance with each other on a weekly basis. This vehicle can be used to help students gain an understanding of their behavior and the behavior of others. Students and teachers have the opportunity to increase their understanding of a variety of current issues. This format builds upon a helping relationship and appropriate ego supports to foster growth in the student's ability to be responsible.

Frequently, in a counseling situation when discussing areas

of responsibility, a student is unable to understand or accept the burden of responsibility. In spite of this, it should be emphasized, discussion is essential to the possible growth in understanding by the student. Perhaps a conversation between the student and teacher will yield results several months hence.

2. *Modeling* – One of the fundamental means of acquiring new behaviors and maintaining existing behaviors is through the use of modeling. Bandura (1969) indicates that "…virtually all learning phenomena resulting from direct experiences can occur on a vicarious basis through observation of other persons' behavior and its consequences for them." The key phrase to bear in mind is, "and its consequences for them." This stresses the notion that behavior is controlled or influenced by its consequences. It seems reasonable to assume that faculty will reinforce behavior that is appropriate, especially if faculty feel the student is performing a preferred response by imitating more appropriate peer models.

Browning and Stover (1971) indicate "…that the role of imitation is necessary in the acquisition of appropriate social behaviors in the residential center." Students learn by observing and "copying" the behaviors of "high status" students and faculty members. In fact, it should be constantly remembered that faculty and staff have a certain quality in the eye of the student. Students admire certain staff members and attempt to model their behaviors. A student who successfully "copies" a behavior of a "high status" student receives a potential windfall of social reinforcers from staff, other students, and most importantly, from himself.

3. *Reinforcement* – During the past fifty years, no learning technique has received more attention than reinforcement. In spite of its apparent simplicity and predictability, this technique is frequently used inappropriately by caring adults. In

addition, many adults visualize the process of reinforcement to be no different than bribery. Let us examine that issue at this time. Bribery is the payment, given now, for a behavior or action to be accomplished at a future time. In addition, the term connotes something dishonest or unethical. Reinforcement is the "payment" given after the completion of a behavior or action. Thus, one difference is the temporal sequencing of the payment. The Bribe comes before the behavior and the Reward comes after the behavior. In fact, when you think about it, reinforcement is similar to our paycheck system. We generally get paid for work accomplished. Therefore, we may visualize the reinforcement process as being similar to the work ethic – you work hard to obtain rewards. This concept of positive reinforcement would take the form of Rrs↑, or a response (R) followed by a reinforcing stimulus (rs) increases (↑) the probability of that response occurring again.

Frequently, when discussing reward learning, there exists a confusion regarding the negative reinforcement and punishment. It should be noted that neither technique is able to teach and sustain behavior to the same degree as positive reinforcement. That is, learning that occurs through positive reinforcement develops faster and is sustained longer than learning obtained by the techniques of negative reinforcement or punishment.

The term negative reinforcement was originally developed to describe a series of events that appeared to be the converse of the application of a reward. In fact, the "reward" came when a noxious stimulus was removed. Thus, rather than the application of a reward to increase the frequency of a behavior, this concept of a negative reinforcement would take the form of R-as↑, or a response (R) followed by the removal of an aversive stimulus (-as) increases (↑) the probability of that response occurring again. It is called a reinforcer because it increases (↑) the probability of the response occurring again. It is part of a process that facilitates the acquisition of a behavior.

On the other hand, punishment is visualized as an inhibitor – something that suppresses an existing response. Punishment would be represented conceptually by the formula Ras↓, or a response (R) followed by the application of an aversive stimulus (as) decreases (↓) the probability of that response occurring again. It should be remembered that punishment is an effective learning technique when applied in a judicious manner. The major drawback when using punishment is the potential damage to the self-esteem of the individual being punished.

Positive reinforcement facilitates learning faster than any other learning technique and has the added benefit of strengthening the self-esteem of the individual being rewarded. Therefore, based on the principles of learning and the tenets of good mental health, positive reinforcement is the teaching technique of choice in a special education setting.

4. *Repetition* – Students frequently learn through the simple process of repetition. This process is based on the concept that simply repeating a behavior time and time again will facilitate learning. The success of this method may be attested to by the legions of former students who have learned their multiplication tables using this time-honored method. For some students, this technique can be a reassuring method of learning, while other students may see this as a boring exercise that simply wastes time. In a boarding school setting, this technique relies strongly on structured activities occurring at a prearranged time and in a regular fashion. This reliance on structure and schedule can be comforting to students who lack confidence and self discipline.

It is most likely quite clear that the techniques of teaching are really methods by which students learn behaviors. These methods of learning can be clearly enunciated in laboratory settings. Fortunately, in the real laboratory of the world of everyday living, the methods are often intertwined and very much related. They interact not only with each other, but also with the teacher and student as well. It is precisely for this reason that teaching techniques should only be utilized if they will provide a positive impact on a student's self-esteem.

7

Method

Each student is thoroughly tested in areas of personality, especially self-esteem, and achievement. This testing takes place prior to and during the initial stages of the R.I.S.E. Program.

Each student is assigned a mentor upon admission to Maplebrook School. The mentor meets with the student weekly to discuss the student's progress and other concerns. The mentor reviews the student's daily performance results and records these results on the weekly performance sheet. The mentor meets with the student to review weekly progress and recommends action to the R.I.S.E. Committee. This meeting takes place on Tuesday in order to give the mentor time to review the previous week's (Monday through Friday) results. The mentor forwards a copy of the weekly performance sheet and recommendation to the R.I.S.E. Committee by 3:30 p.m. each Wednesday.

The R.I.S.E. Committee, consisting of a minimum of three staff members, meets each Wednesday to review all weekly performance sheets and mentor recommendations. Based on this information, the committee decides the independence level on which a student is placed and reports the decision to the mentor and the student.

8

Student Expectations

Student responsibility is the hallmark of the R.I.S.E. Program. As students master their responsibilities (student expectations), they demonstrate maturity and self-control. This mastery of self and environment leads to increased self-esteem. The external ego provided by the traditions at Maplebrook is a major source of support and guidance for our students. A listing of all expected behaviors is almost impossible. After months of discussion, the faculty and staff selected the following:

1. All students are responsible for being prepared for school by bringing their ID cards and being appropriately dressed for school.

2. All students are responsible for being prepared for learning by bringing appropriate supplies and homework to classes.

3. All students are responsible for trying to learn, should give a strong effort for learning in each class and exercise good note-taking skills.

4. All students are responsible for interacting appropriately

with faculty, staff and students and will use appropriate language and observe appropriate School behavior.

5. All students are responsible for fully participating in a team sport, by being on time, prepared and showing effort.

6. All students are responsible for being prepared for evening activities by being on time with appropriate supplies.

7. All students are responsible for trying to participate and give a strong effort in each activity.

8. All students are responsible for contributing to the creation of a healthy, caring environment by being helpful to faculty and students.

9. All students are responsible for demonstrating independence in grooming, room care and dormitory chores.

10. All students are expected to perform appropriately on their apprentice jobs.

These behaviors, when mastered by the student, provide a structure conducive to learning and progress in both academic and social areas. As a student exhibits each expected behavior at an assigned activity, the staff member gives a verbal reinforcer and the student earns a pass (point) for meeting his/her responsibility. These points are recorded on daily report cards for each activity and forwarded to the student's assigned mentor. As mentioned above, the mentor meets with his assigned student, discusses the weekly progress, and reports to the R.I.S.E. Committee. (Samples of the forms are contained in the appendix). The R.I.S.E. Committee reviews the information submitted and assigns each student to an Independence Level based on the accumulated total points.

9

R.I.S.E. Independence Levels

Responsibility Guidelines

Rewards and privileges are important incentives for student motivation. Boarding schools have the opportunity to structure these incentives in such a manner as to promote a high degree of interest. The R.I.S.E. system is based on four (4) Independence Levels constructed to contain an increasing number of privileges commensurate with demonstrated student responsibility. The Independence Levels and sample privileges are as follows:

Students earn their R.I.S.E. points by demonstrating appropriate preparedness, effort, and interaction throughout the day. R.I.S.E. Levels are sequential, and include all responsibilities of previous levels.

BEGINNER LEVELS

Orientation

–   Listens to staff and attempts to follow directions with prompting as needed.

- Follows Major School Rules (see p. 4 of Parent/Student Handbook) and behaves in a safe manner with minimal prompting.
- Meets at least once a week with mentor at scheduled time.

Level 2 (2, 2+)

- Follows Major School Rules and behaves in a safe manner with minimal prompting.
- With prompting as required, follows all rules.
- Meets at least once a week with mentor at scheduled time.
- Knowledge of Level 2 responsibilities.

INTERMEDIATE LEVELS

Level 3 (3, 3_2, 3_3, 3_4)

- Follows Major School Rules and behaves in a safe manner with minimal prompting.
- Cares for room, clothing and personal hygiene to the best of their ability with prompting as needed.
- Completes homework to the best of their ability with prompting as needed.
- Follows all additional rules with prompting as required.
- Demonstrates decreasing need for prompting in above items as he/she progresses to the next sublevel.
- Meets at least once a week with mentor at scheduled time.
- Knowledge of Level 3 responsibilities.

ADVANCED LEVEL

Level 4

– Knows and meets his/her responsibilities with minimal redirecting by staff.
– Meets with mentor at scheduled times.
– Knowledge of Level 4 responsibilities.

INDEPENDENT LEVELS

Independent Level students may choose to use a self-evaluation list based on the ten Student Expectation items listed on page 38.

Contract Level

Student, in conjunction with mentor, must complete and submit a R.I.S.E. Contract outlining responsibilities and privileges for signing by mentor, dormitory staff, R.I.S.E. and Head of School. The R.I.S.E. Committee will place Contract on faculty meeting agenda for input from staff on MAJOR issues.

– Knows and assumes his/her responsibilities without prompting or redirection by staff.
– Self-initiates completion of responsibilities.
– Will participate in leadership training program.

Contract+ Level

Student, in conjunction with mentor, will submit to the R.I.S.E. Committee a letter of application addressing level of participation in altruistic behavior/community service, as well as self-responsibility. Student will also ask his/her mentor and two additional staff members to submit letters of recommendation confirming altruistic behavior/community service and student's self-responsibility. (Note: Altruistic behavior refers to acts of kindness, helping others without being asked.)

- Knows and assumes his/her responsibilities without prompting or redirection by staff.
- Self-initiates completion of responsibilities.
- Continues to demonstrate growth in responsibility for self; takes on more responsibilities.
- Participates in leadership training program.
- Demonstrates altruism (acts of kindness, helping others without being asked) on a regular basis.
- Is involved in community service (formal or informal).

R.I.S.E. Independence Levels:

Sample Privileges
(Academic Campus)

BEGINNER LEVELS

Orientation
- Allowance is $4.00 per week.
- Students participate in the apprentice job program.

Level 2 (2, 2+)
All privileges of previous level plus the following:
- Allowance increase to $5.00 per week.

- Students are eligible for off-campus trips on the weekend.*

INTERMEDIATE LEVELS

Level 3 (3, 32, 33, 34)

All privileges of previous levels plus the following:
- Allowance increase to $6.00 per week.
- Students are eligible for off-campus trips on the weekends.*
- Students are eligible to travel and participate in team sport competitions. (New students at Level 2 may participate only if the competition is during the first four weeks of school.)
- Students are eligible to select and rent a video (PG or PG13) to view in the dorm.

ADVANCED LEVEL

Level 4

All privileges of previous levels plus the following:
- Allowance increase to $7.00 per week.
- Students are eligible for off-campus trips on the weekends.*
- Students are eligible to give campus tours to visitors.
- Students are eligible to run for and hold Student Government office.
- Students are eligible to use Contract Room in dorm (if invited by a Contract student) once during a semester.

INDEPENDENT LEVELS

Contract Level

All privileges of previous levels plus the following:

- Allowance increase to $7.50 per week.
- Students are eligible for off-campus trips on the weekends.*
- Students may stay in the dormitory Contract Room (or TV room for Maples and Brook House) 15 minutes later during the week.
- Students are eligible to sleep 2 hours later on Sunday mornings. (Note: Prior notification is required.)
- Students are eligible to spend free time in the Student Center or computer lab when it is open.
- Students are eligible for off-campus activities unaccompanied by staff (such as walking to the Amenia Plaza).
- Students at least 17 years of age, with written permission from parents, may watch R-rated movies at off-campus movie theaters.
- Students are eligible to "call tables" at meals for seconds and dessert.
- Students are eligible to order take-out food from local restaurants for dinner in the dormitory or Student Center.
- Students are eligible to participate in dress-down days.
- Students are eligible to plan a special activity of their choice through the Leadership Group and the Director of Student Activities.
- Students may negotiate additional privileges with the Dean of Students.
- Students are eligible to apply to be a member of the Society of Honor.

- Students are eligible to eat lunch at picnic tables (weather allowing).
- Students are eligible to be a Peer Assistant to a new student (Level 4 would be eligible if slots were still available).
- Students are eligible to apply to the Academic Dean to be a peer tutor during study hall after his/her own homework is completed.
- Students are eligible for an extra phone night per week.

(Contract Probation should include temporary loss of Contract privileges.)

Contract+ Level

All privileges of previous levels plus the following:
- Allowance increase to $8.00 per week.
- Students are eligible for off-campus trips on the weekends.*
- Students are eligible, if approved by the Academic Dean, to have study hall in the dormitory as long as at least one other student or staff is also in dorm and they sign in/out with the Administrator on Duty, or A.O.D. (for safety).
- In addition to dorm study hall eligibility, students are eligible for study hall (by themselves or with other Contract Plus students of the same gender) in the library, computer lab, or vacant classroom without staff present in room. (Note: Students must sign in/out with A.O.D.)
- Students are eligible to have independent time in

dorm during weekend activity time as long as at least one other student or staff is also in dorm (for safety). (Note: Signing up for this time should be done with the Director of Student Activities during normal weekend activity sign-up time.)

- Students are eligible for trips to a variety of Amenia establishments unaccompanied by staff (such as being dropped off at a restaurant). (Note: Signing up for this time should be done with the Director of Student Activities during normal weekend activity sign-up time.)
- Students may use campus laundry facilities to wash their own clothes. (Students must first pass a basic laundry competency test administered by an ILS instructor. If there is room in the schedule the student may request laundry skill instruction during an ILS period.)
- Students are eligible to be a "table proctor" in the dining hall.

*Weekend and special activity trips are filled in descending order starting at Contract Plus until full or through Level 2, whichever occurs first.

10

Student Expectations/ Responsibilities

Points earned for meeting these responsibilities are discussed and recorded on daily R.I.S.E. slips as well as on a Weekly Summary Sheet. Contract Level students may wish to use this list for self-evaluation purposes.

1. **Prepared for School Assembly**
   All students are responsible for being prepared for school by being on time, bringing their ID cards and being appropriately dressed for school assembly.

2. **Class – Prepared**
   All students are responsible for being prepared for learning by bringing appropriate supplies and home-work to class.

3. **Class – Effort**
   All students are responsible for trying to learn.

Students should give a strong effort for learning in each class, take notes when appropriate, and write down homework assignments on assignment calendar.

4. **Class – Interaction**
   All students are responsible for interacting appropriately with faculty, staff and students, and will use appropriate language and observe appropriate School behavior.

5. **Team Sports**
   All students are responsible for fully participating in a team sport, by being on time and prepared, showing effort, and interacting appropriately, including appropriate language and good sportsmanship behavior.

6. **Study Hall/Evening Activity – Prepared**
   All students are responsible for being prepared for evening activities by being on time and ready to participate with appropriate supplies.

7. **Study Hall/Evening Activity – Effort**
   All students are responsible for trying to participate and give a strong effort with each homework assignment or activity.

8. **Study Hall/Evening Activity – Interaction**
   All students are responsible for contributing to the creation of a healthy, caring environment by being helpful and respectful to faculty and students.

9. **Independence/Dormitory**

All students are responsible for demonstrating independence in room care and dormitory chores (weekly assigned dormitory chore, grooming, personal hygiene, and other dormitory responsibilities). All students are also responsible for interacting appropriately, using appropriate language, and demonstrating appropriate dormitory behavior.

10. **Work Performance**

All students are expected to perform appropriately on their apprentice or advanced apprentice jobs, and submit a weekly timecard.

11

Discussion

Since its inception, the results of the R.I.S.E. Program have been both encouraging and rewarding. Faculty report an increase in on-task classroom behavior and a greater student interest in learning. A review of student progress reports indicates more than ninety-five percent of the students are actively involved in the learning process and show excellent signs of motivation in the great majority of their classes. While this success must be shared with the emphasis on learning styles and the efforts of an outstanding faculty, there is no doubt the R.I.S.E. Program has provided the structure and atmosphere where excellent teaching is accepted by motivated students. Dormitory faculty supports these observations and add comments regarding increased student responsibility in the dormitories and during the wide variety of evening enrichment activities. The structure provided in dormitory life is an important ingredient in the process leading to personal responsibility and independence. As students demonstrate a mastery of the tasks of daily living and learn to live in a cooperative manner with others, they begin to recognize they are in control of their lives. This sense of control has led to increased feelings of competence and eventually a more positive view of themselves. Students are excited about the incentive system and are actively striving for success.

Perhaps the most important aspect of the program thus far is the warm and trusting relationships students have developed with their mentors. These weekly meetings have offered students the support of an adult who is concerned about their progress and well being. Further, the knowledge that each mentor has close communication with parents regarding academic, social, and personal progress of students is an important message. The fact that Maplebrook faculty and staff work closely with students, parents, and other professionals to facilitate growth and development is crucial to a student's success.

Measured growth in self-esteem, as judged from the results of the Piers-Harris Test, has presented us with several interesting issues. Although the majority of the students experienced a rise in scores on the testing, statistical significance has not been achieved. Individual differences appear to have been influenced by reading comprehension, a desire to present oneself in a particular light, and the nature of the test itself. Current plans are to examine other instruments that may control these factors and yield a more accurate measure of student perceived self-esteem. Experience has demonstrated that reliance on traditional paper and pencil measures are less than effective in assessing academic achievement in students with learning differences. Perhaps this would also be true of paper and pencil tests of self-esteem. It appears reasonable that measures that include observations from significant others would serve to enhance the accuracy of assessment.

During the past twenty years, Maplebrook staff have conducted workshops and training sessions for thousands of educators. These workshops have explained the theory and implementation of the R.I.S.E. Program. The comments and feedback are wonderfully complimentary and positive, but an objection is always heard – "the R.I.S.E. Program relies on intense communication among faculty, staff, student and parents and we don't have the time." While I wholeheartedly agree with the former, I must vigorously challenge the latter.

Communication is the process of passing information from one person to another. Schools possess two distinct channels – the formal and the informal. Each carries messages from one person to another downward, upward, across and diagonally. Further, the communication can be written or oral. For communication to be most effective, the element of purpose must also be present. There must be a recognition that the communication is necessary to facilitate the growth and development of each student. There is no doubt that communication is the key to the success of the R.I.S.E. Program. In order to communicate effectively with all individuals sharing the responsibility for a student's program, time is most assuredly a factor. In our system, time for meetings necessary for communicating with students, parents, and colleagues is built into the formal structure. Summary sheets, meeting times and other structures have been developed to facilitate quality communication. Any school committed to a system reflecting an accepted philosophical premise can provide the structures necessary to actuate the agreed upon premise. To do so requires a commitment to change, extensive re-training, and quality personnel. Therefore, an objection regarding time possesses no meaning – one simply makes the time required to achieve quality results.

Independent boarding schools are about much more than strong academics. Those of us who have spent considerable time around such places claim that character education is in the very fiber of our schools. This is true of the finest independent schools in our country. In a special needs school like Maplebrook, this aspect of our program must be given substantial attention and thought.

Many years ago when we created the Responsibility Increases Self-Esteem (R.I.S.E.) Program, our major goal was to assist our students in succeeding in mastering the tasks of everyday living – of getting to class on time, being prepared, expending effort and interacting appropriately with others. This program has been, by all standards of measure, a major success. Parents, faculty, and staff have indicated noticeable behavior changes that reflect growth in positive perceptions of self. Test scores, both at Maplebrook and by independent examiners, have demonstrated tremendous growth in self-esteem and academics.

Part II
Program Supports

12

Personal Responsibility: Courage and Tenacity

I remember years ago, standing on a hillside outside of Seoul, Korea one Christmas Eve, amazed that a nineteen-year-old kid from Connecticut could be stationed just thirty miles south of a Communist army. So much had changed that year – Maris broke Ruth's unbreakable record, my invincible father was recovering from a heart attack, the Berlin Wall was erected, John Kennedy was President, my older brother was aboard ship in the Atlantic fulfilling his military obligation after completing medical school, and Chubby Checker was singing "The Twist." I had just spent the day as a volunteer in a hospital for youngsters injured by land mines that filled the rice paddies and woods north of us. It was a cold, clear night and I was on my way to the 48th Mobile Army Surgical Hospital where I was stationed, and I paused to look at the flickering lights of the city.

When I joined the army at seventeen, I had given little or no thought to the future. I had been a poor student at the Jesuit prep school I attended and seemed to, as I now recall, spend a great deal of time avoiding personal accountability for my academic record. In the military I found immediate success, completing a six-month training program to become a medical laboratory technician with the highest grades in the class, receiving rapid promotions to sergeant within twenty months, and passing several proficiency tests in my field, leading to a higher salary and much recognition. The structure in the U.S. Army and performance-based reward system gave me greater confidence and maturity. It was on that hillside above Seoul that I decided to make the commitment to attend college and join a profession that would allow me to help others.

One evening years ago, while driving on Delavergne Hill outside of Amenia, I paused for a moment to view the flickering lights of the town and was reminded of that night on a hillside in Korea more than forty years ago. Later, I thought of a recent graduate who had written me from Arizona. This young man had come to Maplebrook some years ago as a shy, slightly withdrawn, fearful youngster with little confidence in himself. Fortunately, with encouragement and support from his parents, and our faculty, he responded well to the R.I.S.E. Program and the structure of our School. While at Maplebrook, he discovered a desire to become a chef. After graduating from the high school, and three years later, the C.A.P.S. program, he made a commitment to attend a culinary program at a community college near his home, and was on his way to realizing that goal. During an Alumni Weekend he confided, "Doc, once I realized I was the only one holding me back, I knew I would do it." Naturally, I complimented and encouraged him while thinly concealing my feelings of happiness and pride.

Any of us who are parents or educators are concerned about success for our youngsters. We urge, encourage, exhort and even cajole them to achieve the stated goal. When they fall short, we are disappointed and somewhat perplexed as to why they missed the mark. We call into play our human tendency to blame the youngster, the teacher, and ourselves or some set of circumstances peculiar to this particular situation. More often than not, none of these account for the fact that the goal was not achieved. It may simply be the fact that the goal was not the major focus of the youngster. Once the goal is truly internalized and a personal commitment is made, achievement seems to flow more smoothly. This phenomenon was taught to me by a young man who passed away while at home during the summer before his senior year at Maplebrook. His first few years at the School brought some success, but behavior problems and a lack of maturity seemed to prevent him from fully realizing his goals. One evening he had experienced some difficulty with faculty in study hall and later in the dormitory. I summoned him to my office, after calling his parents, and we had a conversation regarding responsibility and maturity. During this "Headmaster's chat," I shared with him my academic difficulties at Fairfield Prep, and some advice I received from my Headmaster. I pointed out that he should take advantage of the opportunities offered at Maplebrook. I urged him to seize the moment – "carpe diem." I finished by reminding him that his parents were both working very hard to pay the tuition and give him the chance to prove himself. That year this young man grew two academic levels, was voted vice president of his class, earned his driver's license and was a leader on both the swim team and the equestrian club. I will never know if the "Headmaster's chat" was a key to his making the major commitment to seize the moment, but I do know that he achieved his goals.

Courage and tenacity are important ingredients for success.

Several years ago, the Admissions Committee had recommended a young lady not be accepted to our School because of severe language deficits. While contemplating my decision, I was urged by her parents to visit her at summer camp two and one-half hours away in Connecticut. One July morning, I traveled to meet this young girl and was immediately struck by her determination and perseverance. Upon returning to campus, I set aside the committee recommendation and accepted the student. After watching her social growth and maturity, my admiration for her courage was only surpassed by my happiness for her success. While she may never be the academic equal to others, she overcame more to achieve her goal.

This is my thirty-seventh year at Maplebrook, and the forty-fourth since I started my career as a staff psychologist at the New York City Occupational Day School. It doesn't seem that long until I look back. The events and places crowd one another, and the years seem too short to have included them all. It is strange what stands out as I reflect upon my years at Maplebrook. I think of a boy making a speech in the dining room. I cannot recall the words, nor the message, but I am able to remember his victory over shyness and nervousness. Then there was the young lady who overcame tremendous speech and language difficulties to deliver a most eloquent farewell to the two hundred assembled at a Maplebrook graduation. I think of a mother, wise and understanding, who guided and nurtured with a sensitivity that blessed her family. I remember a young, bright teacher coming to her first position in a boarding school infused with the energy and fervor that comes only with youth.

Persons like these stand out, and from our meeting I have become stronger and more fulfilled. I doubt that I could get much satisfaction from my position if I did not feel that in some way, perhaps a small way but still a real one, I am helping young people develop character and independence.

Ten years ago I wrote, "I realize that Headmasters are often regarded by those who know them not, as curious, remote individuals who wield in their own limited domain unlimited powers, ogres who keep students in fear and awe, autocrats who make unreasonable demands, unbending disciplinarians who attempt to make students accountable for their actions." This is pure fiction right from the pages of Charles Dickens.

In today's age, a Headmaster is subject to the control of an over-filled appointment book; a person moving in all directions simultaneously in answer to a sob here, a problem there, an emergency everywhere. Nurturing the boy who struggles to overcome his fears, aiding the young lady who is developing strength and character, cooperating with the parent whose understanding was a blessing to her family, and facilitating the development of the new faculty members describe the real work of a Headmaster. Our privilege is to counsel and administer, to teach some and to help others.

Several years ago I visited a class at the start of the school year, and the first student I encountered (who had been here for two years) I hardly recognized. He had grown three inches over the summer, and had developed a poise and confidence beyond our expectations. Later during the fall at field hockey practice, I noticed one of our players on the edge of the practice field, unconcerned and inattentive. Then came sharp words from our coach, and the student quickly became involved in the practice session. Later the coach explained to me that the student, who possessed a great deal of potential, did not have the confidence needed to be competitive, and required much support and encouragement. At season's end, our fledgling team possessed a new star thanks to the vigilant and caring coach and the determination and hard work of a courageous young student.

As I mentioned earlier, the role of Headmaster has changed over the years. This is especially true at Maplebrook. As the School grew and prospered, administrative tasks such as working with local government, spending time with architects, examining insurance bids and dealing with local business leaders, redirected my focus towards the external aspects of Maplebrook. Seeing this develop, the Trustees appointed me as President/CEO in 2000, so I might concentrate on the external affairs of the School, and the Head of School could remain the true educator at Maplebrook.

The transition was difficult because I spent less time in the Academic building and more time off the campus. The responsibility of being a mentor remained the same, and I had the pleasure of being the mentor for a youngster from Brooklyn, New York who came to Maplebrook well below grade level in every subject. With extraordinary determination and focus, this young man earned his Associate's Degree at Dutchess Community College while attending our C.A.P.S. Program. I recently spoke with him and he just earned a B.A. degree in communications.

I am so thankful for the career I have chosen when youngsters "put it all together" and succeed. Success comes in different forms, such as the young woman who graduated in 1991, remained active in Maplebrook's Alumni Association and recently married a young man who did not attend Maplebrook. My wife and I attended their wedding, and it was extremely moving witnessing the true warmth and affection they possessed for each other. This is success at its best. Carpe diem, Kim and Rich.

Most recently, I had the occasion to visit with several alumni. I was singularly impressed with a young lady who graduated several years ago. She told me of her neighborhood activism to convince city officials a traffic light was needed at a dangerous intersection. The process was long and arduous. She spoke of how she was continuing the process and would eventually be successful. Considering the poise and confidence she obtained to this point, she has already achieved her success.

I am so fond of Maplebrook and the memories are so very plentiful. Memories of a young lad driving for a lay-up on the basketball court, a young girl competing to her limit as a member of the swim team, a composite memory of several students achieving beyond their own expectations, conversations with many youngsters, all individually remembered, who struggled to overcome self-doubt and painful discouragement. As I reflect over my own career, I am grateful that I have been given the talents and temperament to teach. I am held inescapably by the whole exciting process of growth and development and by the limitless nature of the human potential.

My feelings are both joyous and humbling. Joyous in seeing the success of the R.I.S.E. Program, but also humbling in thinking of some of the virtues the students possess that, at times, I have not fully mastered. Recently a young lady who earned her high school diploma decided to return for a post-graduate year in order to strengthen her study skills so that she might succeed when she would attend college the next year. In making this decision, she demonstrated a degree of patience I often find elusive as I strive to actualize particular goals. She has shown me the wisdom of Tolstoy's words in War and Peace, "The strongest of all warriors are these two – time and patience."

13

Social Skills and Learning Disabilities

Until 1990, the bulk of educational advances with individuals with learning disabilities was in the area of academics. Methodology was emphasized through techniques such as Orton-Gillingham, Slingerland, or strategies such as cognitive mapping, whole language approach, and multisensory teaching. Only since 1990 or so has there been any attention expended on the social aspects of learning disabilities.

Many youngsters with learning disabilities experience great difficulty in social adjustment. Research has indicated many youngsters with learning disabilities display mild to moderate problems in social relations and emotional stability. Some intervention must be made to assist these youngsters. Unfortunately, determining which techniques are most effective with youngsters with learning disabilities has been an elusive process.

In the past decade, the most promising methods have been teaching organizational strategies and cognitive behavior modification to children with learning disabilities. Both of these methods place the responsibility for the change on the student, not the parent or teacher. This is important because according to Epanchin & Paul (1987), longitudinal studies indicate that learning disabilities do not disappear, rather, many of these children develop behavioral and social problems that complicate their adult adjustment.

Now I will discuss some reasons why this occurs and interventions that appear to have helped some youngsters overcome their difficulties. Children with learning disabilities are described as socially less desirable than normally achieving children (Bryan & Bryan, 1983). In a series of studies of sociometric ratings – these are ratings of how popular other children in the class are by all children in that class – LD children are consistently rated as less desirable. Some reasons are:

- They are less predictable
- They complain all the time
- They have difficulty interacting
- They don't know how to play
- They have poor self-concepts
- They do poorly in sports
- They achieve poorly
- They "look" a little different

14

Selective Attention

Why does this occur? Many theories have been postulated as to the etiology of these behaviors. The theory with most promise in recent years has focused on selective attention in learning: the ability to focus on the critical information that facilitates learning while disregarding extraneous information that does not help in learning. This process has to do with the way we think about thinking and is influenced by prior experiences. To illustrate this process consider the following:

The figure below contains nine dots. Please connect each of the nine dots with four, or less, straight lines without retracing any line and without taking the pencil off the paper.

Most of us have difficulty in solving this problem because of prior conditioning. What do we see – one large square, four smaller squares, three rows of three dots, or three columns of three dots?

The problem states there are nine dots. Our prior conditioning permits us to see the nine dots in the context of a large square, within which we may perceive other geometric configurations. It is the essence of "squareness" which we have seen much of our lives that hinders our solution to this problem. We attempt to arrive at the solution within the confines of the square as in the following incorrect attempts:

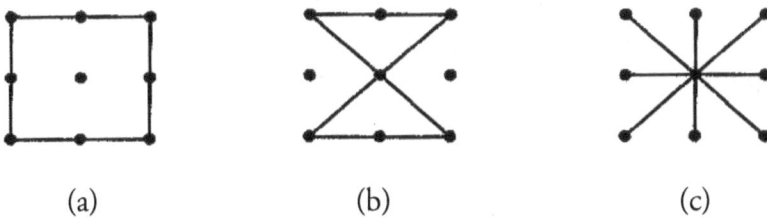

(a)   (b)   (c)

To complete (a), one omits the center dot. Attempt (b) necessitates the omission of the two dots to the right and to the left of center. Finally, attempt (c) is only possible by raising the pencil from the paper.

The solution is only possible by perceiving the figure as nine dots without the characteristic of squareness. We must attempt to solve the problem by exceeding the confines of the square.

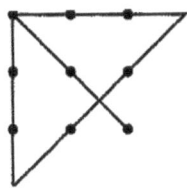

This becomes difficult to solve because we see more than nine dots. All our experiences in life have influences on our thinking. From our earliest pre-memory as an infant in a crib staring up at the ceiling, we have learned the essence of shape. We see this as a square and attempt to solve the problem within that preconceived configuration. In order to solve the problem, we must learn a new way of looking at the nine dots. We must break out of the concept that confines our thinking.

The same principle applies to our youngsters as they view themselves. They have experienced many failures since starting school, both in academics and in social situations. They have been frequently corrected and scolded throughout these failures. They are not as good as their peers in academics, in sports, and in other aspects of everyday life. When they look in the mirror they do not like what they see. This is a painful process.

Some youngsters withdraw and give up trying to succeed, others become angry, and others create false personas that enable them to accept themselves a little better. All develop a certain degree of egocentrism; whereby, others are responsible for their failures and this leads to the type of thinking where society must adapt while they abdicate their responsibility.

15

Cognitive Behavior Modification and R.I.S.E.

Youngsters with learning problems have profited from a technique called cognitive behavior modification (Meichinbaum, 1977). This technique requires a youngster to be aware of the nature of the intervention because this leads to self-monitoring and self-feedback. This technique is often referred to as experiential learning, and is one of the many tools used in the Responsibility Increases Self-Esteem (R.I.S.E.) program utilized at Maplebrook School. The heart of the program is based on the premise that individuals are responsible for their own behavior and if they are to become independent and "fit into" society, they must recognize their responsibility and be deeply involved in monitoring their own behavior.

The R.I.S.E. Program is a highly structured system in which we create a therapeutic learning environment. This is done by emphasizing the quality of daily interactions and helping students develop the social skills to enhance their ability to deal with everyday events that occur in their environment, accentuating the importance of people and providing a support system.

The mentor system, the centerpiece of this program, is intended to facilitate each student to achieve their educational, social, and life skills goals. The professional staff are specially trained in ego supportive counseling techniques, based on the work of Carl Rogers and later Al Trieschman. As explained in the earlier section on Ego Development, shared ego is affected by giving support and indicating that together (the student and mentor) will find a solution. External ego is affected by using the rules, regulations and structure of the School environment. Ego components are best used by structuring events in which the strengths of the students are utilized, and group ego represents a sort of "esprit de corps." The faculty meet in individual counseling sessions with each student once or twice a week to review their progress. At these sessions, they discuss student progress as reported in daily achievement logs submitted by faculty and counselors. Also discussed are strategies to increase the students' probability of success. The student and mentor submit weekly progress reports to the R.I.S.E. Committee for their review. The committee makes recommendations for special awards, commendations and recognition. In addition, the committee, based on the student's progress, assigns each student to an "independence level." These levels have been carefully designed so that the greater the progress, the higher the independence level and the lower the amount of staff supervision.

Each year's results note significant increases in self-esteem. In addition, substantial increases in responsible behavior appear to be facilitating student growth in both academic and social areas.

16

Experiential Learning in R.I.S.E.

The student has a concrete personal experience, reflects on it, either alone or with his/her mentor, then formulates a general concept or basic principle to guide him/her in future situations, and formulates an alternate behavior to test out in new situations. After testing the new behavior, the process of reflection continues.

Both cognitive behavior modification and strategic training depend on the youngster's awareness of the process that is being imposed upon him/her. The youngster becomes an integral part of the intervention. This active participation, in itself, may be the most important element of success. In fact, this empowers the youngster to take control over his/her own life. Isn't this what we desire for our children? How independent can an 18-year-old become when we tell him what to eat, what to wear, and when to go to bed?

How much damage to a youngster's self-esteem do we cause when we "outlaw" coffee at breakfast because he/she can't "handle" it? How much confidence do we build by finding excuses for the student's lack of effort in learning? How much inappropriate learning do we teach when we allow youngsters to interrupt a conversation?

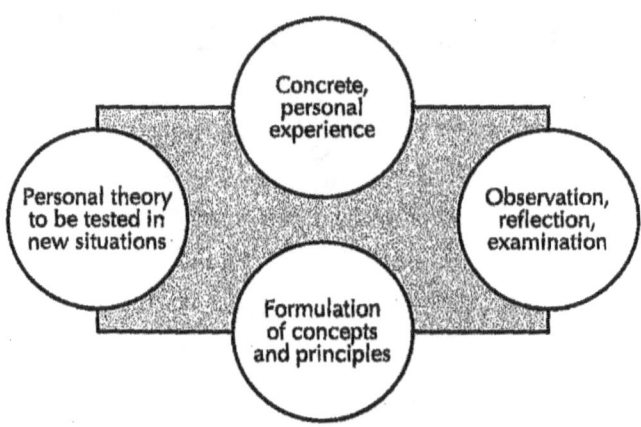

The area of learning disabilities has been floundering for many years in search of effective intervention strategies. Emphasis on improving academic performance has been at the expense of developing social skills programs. The R.I.S.E. Program, developed in 1988, has attracted considerable attention in many circles and has proven effective in enhancing the learning of social skills. The basic principle is clear. To produce more self-directed independent individuals, it is necessary to give more opportunity to practice self-direction.

17

Social Misperception Syndrome

Social Misperception Syndrome is a well-chronicled phenomenon affecting a great number of individuals with learning disabilities. Educators and other professionals have, in the past, focused mainly on the academic aspects of learning disabilities (Wilchesky & Reynolds, 1986). During the past decade, there has been an increased interest in such non-academic areas as social skills acquisition (Spafford & Grosser, 1991), generalization of social skills (Misra, 1992), self-determination (Schoss, Alper & Hayne, 1993), and self-concept (Fazzone, 1990 and Adelman & Taylor, 1990). In an excellent article synthesizing research defining the social problems of some children with learning disabilities, Spafford & Grossser (1993) discuss the impact of family, school, and environment on personality development of both children and adults with learning disabilities. In their view, new findings in neurophysiology negate, to a large extent, traditional emphases on family dysfunction, school failure, or personality disturbances as primary causes of the social problems of children with learning disabilities. If this hypothesis is correct, then it would be reasonable to consider a didactic approach in the acquisition of social skills.

The quality of life is in large part determined by our interpersonal and small group relationships. A major portion of our lives is spent in various kinds of small group situations. We do not exist as solitary human beings but as members of families, activity groups, teams, classes, clubs and circles of friends. Vital to membership in such groups is the ability to communicate in a clear and productive manner. Communicating in small groups is so much a part of our lives that most of us take it for granted. We fail to realize that many individuals with a learning disability have difficulty with proper interpersonal interactions on an individual basis. This difficulty is magnified when placed in the context of small group interaction. These individuals have difficulty perceiving and understanding what is happening in these groups. In effect, they need to learn the skills necessary to be productive members of a group.

As mentioned above, the experiential learning model requires reflection and examination in order to be effective. It is difficult to examine an issue in a vacuum. This is especially true for teenagers who require the support and approval of their peers. In an effort to stimulate a more penetrating examination of the variety of social skills practiced by youngsters with learning difficulties, the study or learning group approach was utilized. According to Brilhart (1987), "These groups are similar to encounter or therapy groups to the extent that they are formed as a medium of learning and growth for the participants." The ego supports provided by such a group can be a tremendous catalyst for discussion and feedback.

Teen Awareness groups were initiated in 1989 to provide a forum for student discussion and reflection of a variety of issues they deem important. The group structure consisted of a counselor/psychologist meeting with six to eight students for one hour per week. The issues to be discussed were determined by the group and the counselor's role was to facilitate discussion and reflection. The popularity of the group led to a second social support, more didactic in nature, designed to help the students understand the nature of learning disabilities.

In 1991 an enrichment course was developed based on the book, *The Survival Guide for Kids with LD*. The course was offered one day per week for 12 weeks. The course description taken from the back jacket of this excellent text by Fisher and Cummings (1990) is as follows:

"Kids with LD are smart and can learn.

They just learn *differently*.

If you're a kid with LD – or if you're a parent or teacher of a child with LD – then you probably have a lot of questions about LD.

Questions like: Why do some people have LD? How do people get LD? Are there different kinds of LD? Why does LD make it so hard to learn? What goes on in LD programs and LD rooms? Does LD ever go away? What happens to kids with LD when they grow up? Can a person with LD go to college?

Look inside to find out:
- Ten ways to get along better in school
- Tips for making and keeping friends
- Eight ways to get along better at home
- What happens when you grow up
- How YOU can be a winner and much more!

Special sections list learning resources for kids with LD, give tips on home and homework, and point the way to organizations that provide additional information and support."

This course provides a wonderful framework for students to understand a bit more about learning differences in general and, through classroom discussions, their particular learning problem. This experience helps students to attend to what they know best, namely, themselves. They are always too willing to offer opinions on others; perhaps the process of learning more about themselves will facilitate becoming open and honest with themselves. This will lead to a self disclosure and truthfulness necessary to promote growth. But the question of personal growth always comes down to the question of when the student really wishes to change? Ultimately, this question can only be answered by the individual student, but I have little doubt that the knowledge one acquires about himself/herself is a healthy impetus in the direction of change.

Individual responsibility contains an obligation to be a responsible member of today's complex society. In order to function in a responsible manner within the larger context of society, individuals must have appropriate skills. To address this issue, a major addition to the R.I.S.E. Program was initiated in 1993.

18

Interpersonal Psychology

Socialization is a far-reaching term, an exact definition of which can be both confusing and elusive. Human beings begin life as rather dependent egocentric creatures. They are concerned primarily with the satisfaction of their own needs and the speed with which these needs are satisfied. During the early years of life, children move from this self-centeredness to a more interactive state of being. They begin to seek and enjoy the companionship of others, as well as begin to develop a variety of skills, abilities, and strategies necessary to become an autonomous and independent individual. Many factors influence the acquisition and mastery of the social skills necessary to be fully integrated into today's complex society. Among the factors frequently mentioned as partial determinants of social skills acquisition are child-rearing, social class, cultural differences, genetics, intelligence, learning and peer influences.

Adolescents' social skills acquisition is generally a reflection of the ability to think about thinking. They develop the ability of conceptualizing the thoughts of others, along with their own. They recognize that they are interactive social beings functioning in a society. Youngsters who have not fully developed these concepts are in need of specific training in order to acquire the ability to interact as a member of society successfully.

Youngsters possessing mild to moderate learning problems with associated cognitive limitations tend to be deficient in important social skills. Further, research has proven (Schumaker, Hazel, Pedersen, 1988) these social skills can be taught with appropriate instruction. Schumaker indicates, "Without acceptable social skills, young people have great difficulty interacting successfully in school, at home, and on the job. Repeated failures in the social realm can create a self-defeating pattern of discouragement and isolation." The R.I.S.E. Program has been designed to promote success and thereby increase positive feelings about oneself.

During the first six years of implementation, faculty and parents have noted the many positive impacts the R.I.S.E. Program has had on students. Unfortunately, our observations have included the fact that there appears to be a major problem in the generalization of particular social behaviors. After much discussion and thought, it was decided to expand the scope of R.I.S.E. to include formal instruction in the area of interpersonal interaction. To accomplish this task, we decided to adapt the Social Skills for Daily Living program developed at the University of Kansas Institute for Research in Learning Disabilities. The authors indicate, "Social Skills for Daily Living presents a proven, effective method of increasing students' appropriate performance of social skills. By working through this curriculum, students can expect to significantly improve their effectiveness in a variety of social situations." Our goal is to integrate the monitoring of the results of the formal instruction within the structure of the R.I.S.E. Program.

In response to the need for a didactic affiliate to the R.I.S.E. Program, a basic course in social skills acquisition was created as follows:

Interpersonal Psychology I

Course Description

The Interpersonal Psychology course presents important concepts and skills of social interaction. By working through this course, students can expect to significantly improve their effectiveness in a variety of social situations. The course is a comprehensive program of thirty different skills in the general areas of conversation and friendship skills, skills for getting along with others, and problem solving skills. Students develop skills through reading, writing, memorizing, and a great deal of role playing.

Course Objectives

To understand and use appropriate basic behavioral components in social interactions, including the following: facing the other person, maintaining eye contact, using appropriate voice, tone, facial expression and body posture.

To understand and use appropriate conversation and friendship skills, including the following: active listening, greetings, saying goodbye, answering questions, asking questions, introducing yourself, interrupting, conversational skills and making friends.

To understand and use skills for getting along with others, including the following: accepting thanks, giving thanks, accepting compliments, apologizing, accepting "no", resisting peer pressure, responding to teasing, accepting criticism and giving criticism.

To understand and use problem solving skills, including the following: following instructions, getting help, asking for feedback, giving rationales, solving problems, persuasion, negotiation, joining group activities, starting activities with others and giving help.

General Education Objective Met by the Course

In addition to acquiring the basic knowledge and skills for understanding interpersonal psychology, the student will be exposed to a variety of learning opportunities such as: small and large group instruction, cooperative learning, role playing, communication skills and the ability to follow directions.

Outline of Course Content

Body Basics	Using the appropriate behavioral components in social interactions. These components include facing the other person, maintaining eye contact, and using an appropriate voice, tone, facial expression, and body posture.
Active Listening	Listening closely and asking questions to make sure one understands what others are saying.
Greeting	Saying "hello" or "hi" and asking a question when one first sees someone or wants to meet someone.
Saying Goodbye	Ending conversations in a friendly way and then leaving.

Answering Questions	Responding appropriately, honestly and with a complete statement when asked a question.
Asking Questions	Asking questions when needed; for example, to get more information, to find out how to do something, or to clarify instructions.
Introducing Yourself	Saying one's name and, if appropriate, shaking hands when meeting others.
Interrupting	Breaking into or joining a conversation appropriately, without being rude and without talking when others are talking.
Conversational Skills	Being able to carry on a conversation, including interrupting appropriately, greeting the other person, introducing oneself, listening, asking and answering questions, and saying goodbye.
Making Friends	Being able to make friends with whom one has things in common. Able to orchestrate a series of relationship-building encounters, including greeting the person, having conversations, and initiating activities.
Accepting Thanks	Listening to thanks and accepting thanks appreciatively.
Saying Thanks	Thanking others sincerely and appreciatively.
Accepting Compliments	Listening to compliments and accepting them sincerely.
Giving Compliments	Sincerely complimenting others when they have done something well or look especially nice.

Apologizing	Apologizing for mistakes and offering to make amends in an appropriate way.
Accepting "No"	Accepting no for an answer, especially from authority figures, without arguing.
Resisting Peer Pressure	Saying no to peers when they suggest a wrong or illegal activity. Able to suggest an alternate activity and/or gracefully get out of an activity if necessary without losing friends.
Responding to Teasing	Handling teasing appropriately by remaining calm, making statements appropriate to the situation, and refraining from fighting.
Accepting Criticism	Listening to and trying to understand criticism without getting angry. Making appropriate statements regarding how one will try to change.
Giving Criticism	Explaining to others in a calm, concerned way how they have upset someone.
Following Instructions	Listening to instructions and accurately carrying them out pleasantly and without argument.
Getting Help	Asking for help from appropriate people when needed.
Asking for Feedback	Asking an appropriate person to analyze the quality of one's work and give suggestions for improving it.
Giving Rationales	Giving good reasons for doing or

	believing something, emphasizing the benefits to the other person.
Solving Problems	Being able to analyze a problem, develop possible solutions, choose the best solution, and specify a plan for carrying out the chosen solution.
Persuasion	Trying to convince others to agree with something or to do what one wants by giving good rationales.
Negotiation	When having a conflict, engaging in a series of interchanges to forge a compromise and reach an agreement with the other person.
Joining Group Appropriately	Approaching a group member appropriately and asking to join an ongoing group activity.
Starting Activities with Others	Initiating activities with others and making the necessary arrangements.
Giving Help	Assisting others when needed, without taking over the task. Able to teach others new skills.

Instructional Methods and Evaluation

Teaching methods include class lectures, demonstrations, role playing, student reading and student presentations. Specific teaching techniques include direct instruction, multisensory presentations, video-taping, modeling, role playing and positive reinforcement.

Individual student requirements are indicated in each student I.E.P. Students will be evaluated on their performance in class activities, class assignments, homework, projects and teacher constructed texts.

Determination of Final Grade

The student will be evaluated on the goals and objectives of his/her I.E.P. Grades will be determined according to the achieved average percentage of accuracy in relationship to the objectives of the I.E.P., via use of teacher constructed tests, teacher evaluation of performance on class activities homework and projects. The text will be materials from Social Skills for Daily Living Program, American Guidance Service, Circle Pine, Minnesota.

Within the past years there have been some changes implemented in the Interpersonal Psychology curriculum. Interpersonal Psychology I is an introduction to the concepts and skills of social interaction. Interpersonal Psychology II was developed to build upon the introductory course by including certain topics that are vital to each student's full social growth, in such a way as to allow the students to practice each skill outside the classroom.

Interpersonal Psychology II

Course Description

Interpersonal Psychology will give students an awareness of important concepts and skills in social interaction. The course presents to the student concise methods to significantly improve his/her effectiveness in a variety of social situations.

Interpersonal Psychology II covers different skills necessary for social awareness, and is an extension of Interpersonal Psychology I.

INTERPERSONAL PSYCHOLOGY

Statement of Course Objectives

- Develop and improve the students' awareness of themselves and how their self-esteem is a contributing factor to this awareness.
- Recognize and use relevant vocabulary.
- Improve reading comprehension.
- Recognize patterns in relationships and how to improve relationships.
- Enhance student respect for himself/herself and others.
- Improve problem solving and goal setting skills.
- Develop and use ways to handle criticism.

General Education Objectives Met by the Course

The student will develop an awareness of himself/herself and acquire the basic knowledge and social skills for understanding interpersonal psychology. The student will be exposed to a variety of learning opportunities such as: small and large group instruction, cooperative learning, independent study, and hands-on conferencing. Interpersonal Psychology II is designed to develop communication, social skills, and enhance the ability to follow directions.

Outline of Course Content

Self-Awareness

Self-Esteem	Realizing what self-esteem is, how
Evaluation	students see themselves, and which aspects they would like to improve.

Communication Skills

Body Language	Learning to use and read body language appropriately in order to communicate the correct messages.
Non-Verbal Messages	Learning to read and effectively use nonverbal messages.
"I" Statements	Stating and owning your feelings without attacking the other person.
Listening	Actively listening and hearing what someone is saying to avoid communication blocks and misunderstandings.
Interrupting and Timing	Joining a conversation appropriately and learning when to interrupt with important information.
Conversational Skills	Reading and interpreting communication cues that help initiate or end a conversation, as well as ways to maintain conversation.

Relationship Skills

Friendships and Relationships	Recognizing the different types of relationships and friendships, as well as characteristics of each and how to make and maintain certain relationships.
Control	Learning how and when to set boundaries and the importance of respect for others.
Rejection and Attitudes	Learning how to deal with rejection in relationships and why it is important to have a good attitude and avoid gossiping.

Criticism and Attitudes

Accepting Criticism	Listening and trying to understand criticism without getting angry.
Giving Criticism	Explaining to others how they have upset someone and how to relay the message appropriately.
Self-Criticism	Recognizing and understanding reasons we need to change and ways to remain positive in assessing the things we need to change.
Constructive Criticism	Recognizing the difference between constructive ways to criticize and insulting someone.
Assets and Limitations	Accentuating assets without bragging and accepting those limitations that cannot be changed.

Problem Solving Skills

Anger vs. Fear	Recognizing anger and not mistake it for fear. How to resolve anger and deal with fear.
Stress Management	Recognizing the different types of conflicts and how to avoid turning them into stressful situations.
Emotions	Recognizing how to handle emotions properly and recognize the proper emotion to a particular situation.
Passive/Aggressive Or Assertive	Recognizing when it is appropriate to be passive, aggressive, or assertive and take responsibility for actions and decisions.

Decision Making and Goal Setting

Taking Risks	Recognizing when it is a good time to take a risk and how to weigh the pros and cons to a decision.
Making Choices	Exploring all options before making an important decision.
Commitment	Standing by a decision that is made and living up to a commitment that is made through trust.
Internet Safety	Understanding the positive and negative aspects of the Internet.

These skills include using social networking sites appropriately, learning what a "friend" is related to the Internet when there is not face-to-face contact, awareness of the levels of privacy, recognizing cyber-bullying in all aspects of Internet use (texts, social media sites, etc.)

Instructional Methods and Evaluation

Teaching methods include lectures, one-to-one and group discussions, journal writings, visual aids, multisensory presentations, modeling, role playing, in- and out-of-class projects, and computer instruction. Individual requirements as they are indicated on each student's I.E.P. will be exercised throughout the course. Each student will be evaluated based on performance in class, assignments, projects, and tests.

Determination of Final Grade

The student will be evaluated on the goals and objectives

of his/her I.E.P. Grades will be determined according to the achieved average percentage of accuracy in relationship to the objectives of the I.E.P., via use of teacher constructed tests, teacher evaluation of performance on class activities, homework, and projects.

Texts

A wide variety of texts with reproducible pages are used during Interpersonal Psychology.

Doody, Mary J. and Janet M. Dick, *Fast Forward: A Self-Esteem Program.*

Karsten, Mary, *Developing Healthy Self-Esteem in Adolescents.*

Scully, Jennifer, *The Power of Social Skills in Character Development.*

The implementation of this adaptation to the R.I.S.E. Program takes place within the structure of the school day. This course was developed using the Social Skills for Daily Living curriculum. Each student enrolled at the School is required to successfully complete the course. The course requires three hours per week of instruction for an entire semester. Students not mastering the goals and objectives within this time frame are enrolled for an additional semester.

The entire staff is briefed on the content, goals and objectives of the course. Using the "interaction" sections of the R.I.S.E. Program, they are asked to observe the students' appropriate application of course material. Daily reports are sent to the students' mentors for review. Mentors are encouraged to discuss progress with each student on a weekly basis.

This revision of the R.I.S.E. Program will be measured by staff observation and reports from parents. In addition, "interaction" scores will be matched with course grades in an attempt to examine the relationship between knowledge of the social skills material and application of this same material in everyday interactions.

19

Character Education

Over the years, the combined efforts to implement the R.I.S.E. Program and develop the social skills class experience led the faculty to develop a Character Education Initiative. Based on the 1991 book *Education for Character*, by Thomas Lickona, the School set about the task of re-tooling the culture of the School.

The first step was to train the entire staff, from the Headmaster to the support personnel. To initiate the process, the executive leadership enrolled in a college-sponsored course regarding the teaching of respect and responsibility in schools. In addition, Mr. Gary Fitzherbert, former Headmaster of Devereux Glenholme School and a leading proponent of the "Character Counts" movement, conducted training for the entire staff.

The second step involved the selection of core values to be embraced by the entire Maplebrook community. To accomplish this task, a small committee of faculty and staff distributed a questionnaire to parents, staff, students, and Trustees. The results yielded agreement on eight values. These eight pillars of character comprise our students' goals: Respect, Caring, Trust,

Faith, Work Ethic, Fairness, Responsibility, and Citizenship. Over time the eight core values became totally intertwined with the R.I.S.E. Program and part of the "culture of the School."

The third step was to examine existing programs and activities to see which might have opportunities to reinforce one or more of the eight core values.

The final step was to establish new programs that would provide opportunities to learn the core values and/or reinforce the performance of one or more of the eight pillars.

Programs/Activities That Reinforce Character Education

Chaplaincy Services. Since 2000, Maplebrook has added a full time Chaplain to the staff. This individual is available to every student or parent regardless of his or her religious preference. The Chaplain is there to counsel, help with bereavement issues, and tend to the spiritual needs of our students. In addition, all religious holidays are celebrated at the School and explained to all the students/staff by the Chaplain.

Awards are an integral part of most school programs. These range from teacher awards for classroom effort and performance to sports awards given by coaches for a student's progress on the playing field and lead to school-wide awards given in recognition of stellar effort and performance in all aspects of school life. At Maplebrook, the "major" awards are given during graduation, where almost 300 individuals gather to witness youngsters receiving Maplebrook's highest award – a high school diploma. In addition, select students receive the following awards:

The Mark Metzger Citizenship Award given to students who

excel in modeling good character, community service and who possess an altruistic attitude.

The David Brachfeld Award given in memory of this student, who died while on summer vacation prior to his senior year. The Academic Program Student Center is dedicated to David and his determination as exemplified by the Latin phrase from Horace – carpe diem – seize the day. David took full advantage of his Maplebrook experience in his final year at our School. He became Vice President of the Student Government, a valued member of the Swim Team and Equestrian Club, portrayed Franklin Delano Roosevelt in the school play, earned his driver's license, and most importantly, grew two academic levels in one year on standardized testing.

The Jonathan Swartwood Award given each year to two undergraduates in memory of Jonathan, who graduated in 1972. This award is presented to students who exemplify the true Maplebrook philosophy of friendship and independence.

The Graduate Award presented to the outstanding male and female graduates who, in the eyes of the faculty, have excelled in overall performance of academics, social skills, and independence.

Society of Honor Member Recognition. At Maplebrook, we take great pride in educating the whole person. Maplebrook educates the mind through challenging academics; educates the body through rigorous sport; and educates the heart by providing good role models and programs that reinforce universally accepted values and moral principles. The Character Education Committee established an Honor code, which entails the following:

- To be honest and loyal
- To treat people with kindness and dignity

- To respect all members of the school community
- To take academic and personal responsibilities seriously
- To be involved in the life of the school
- To respect all personal and school property
- To try to be the best one can be in all areas
- To conduct oneself in an appropriate manner and abide by all the rules
- To be a good role model.

Students who exemplify all aspects of this Honor Code can be nominated and elected to the Maplebrook Society of Honor. There is an application process whereby a student writes a character statement explaining why he/she would like to be in the Society of Honor. This statement includes any community service, offices held through Student Government and examples of altruistic behavior. The students then must obtain three (3) letters of recommendation from his/her mentor, a faculty member living in the dormitory and a teacher. Once a student's application is complete, the Character Education Committee will elect appropriate candidates to the Society of Honor. Elected members are awarded a $2,000 scholarship toward the following year's tuition.

Once a new "class" of honorees is elected, there is a special induction ceremony held in the chapel. All faculty and staff attend and if possible, the student's parents. The feeling of pride and accomplishment permeates the whole ceremony as already established Society of Honor members usher in the new inductees, participate in the reading of the honor code and officially welcome the new members. After a prayer for the inductees and the whole school community, mentors complete the ceremony by presenting each inductee with honor cords and a Society of Honor pin. Candles are lit and the ceremony is completed with a processional of current and new Society of Honor members. The entire school community gathers for a special recognition dinner in the Dining Hall where together we can celebrate the achievements of our School's student leaders.

Community Service. Giving back to one's community is an integral part of building good character. At Maplebrook, community service is a voluntary activity so as to embrace the altruistic spirit. When community service is required as part of graduation, then it simply becomes "one more thing I have to do". We have built a community service program that not only teaches the students to give back, but teaches a larger lesson for independence. If people in your community know you, or recognize you, they will be more willing to help when you need it. Besides, the wonderful feelings that are produced by helping others are reward enough. Some examples of community service projects include, but are not limited to: Hand-in-Hand 5K Run/Walk that raises funds for a local speech and language center, Adopt-a-Family for the Holidays where money, clothing and toys are collected for a needy family and Sunday in the Country food drive whereby students collect money for the local food bank at Thanksgiving. Activities such as the Adopt-A-Highway Program or singing holiday carols at the local senior citizens complex all build character just by their very nature of helping others. There are many others and specialized community service projects are welcome. Teddy bears and mosquito netting were sent back with a student from Nigeria, boxes of supplies were sent to Afghanistan for the K-9 soldiers during the war and funds were raised after Hurricane Katrina.

Community service is not limited to the Maplebrook

campus. Approximately half of the student body is a member of the local Lion's Club as LEO Club members. This is the student version of our community's Lion's Club and they are called upon to help with various projects throughout the community at large. Not only are they sought out because of the helpful reputation they have established, but they are well-respected members of our local community.

Learning and teaching is much more than awards. In a boarding school, "every moment is a teaching moment." Therefore, every activity has the potential to be a teaching activity for some aspect of our eight pillars of character: activities such as community service and team sports also present a plethora of opportunities for teaching and learning character, as do peer tutoring, saying grace before meals, dormitory chores and involvement in student government.

20

Bullying

The facts on bullying demonstrate it is a growing problem among teens and children. There are several different types of bullying including cyber bullying, bullying in schools, verbal bullying, social bullying, and physical bullying.

Bullying can happen anywhere. Many children and teens are regular victims of bullying which can lead to serious emotional issues, as well as, problems with self-esteem and self-image. For our purposes we will look closer at bullying in schools. Ron Banks of The Educational Resource Information Center of the United States Department of Education summarized the problem in February 2013 by stating:

> "Bullying in schools is a worldwide problem that can have negative consequences for the general school climate and for the right of students to learn in a safe environment without fear. Bullying can also have negative lifelong consequences--both for students who bully and for the victims. Although much of the formal research on bullying has taken place in the Scandinavian

countries, Great Britain, and Japan, the problems associated with bullying have been noted and discussed wherever formal school environments exist.

Bullying is comprised of direct behaviors such as teasing, taunting, threatening, hitting, and stealing that are initiated by one or more students against a victim. In addition to direct attacks, bullying may also be more indirect by causing a student to be socially isolated through intentional exclusion. While boys typically engage in direct bullying methods, girls who bully are more apt to utilize these more subtle indirect strategies, such as spreading rumors and enforcing social isolation (Ahmad & Smith, 1994; Smith & Sharp, 1994). Whether the bullying is direct or indirect, the key component of bullying is that the physical or psychological intimidation occurs repeatedly over time to create an ongoing pattern of harassment and abuse."

In a boarding school environment bullying can affect the school day, as well as, after school activities. Since boarding schools are more insular in nature than attending a regular public school, there is a greater opportunity to control (influence) the environment to eliminate bullying. Haber (2007) defines bullying as "a repeated and/or chronic pattern of hurtful behavior including intent to maintain an imbalance of power: for example, when one individual finds satisfaction in harming people whom he/she considers weaker to build up his/her own sense of power. Bullying is not about working out a conflict, and it isn't between evenly matched opponents." Haber goes on to indicate "it isn't between evenly matched opponents. It crosses the line into unequal power dynamics where one person wants to control another. The bully believes the target is weaker in some way, whether that's physical, mental, social, emotional, or a combination. Bullies get satisfaction from harming their targets." Please keep in mind that the difference between bullying and fighting is the issue of power. Fighting is simply an escalation of conflict and is normal. Kids can argue and yell and scream at each other and may even shove or resort to fisticuffs without possessing a bullying element to it.

Since 1988 the R.I.S.E. program has proved to be an effective tool to reduce and yes even eliminate bullying. The structure of the program is based on the principle of operant conditioning which is a naturally positive approach. The program stresses positive character traits emphasizing the concept of altruism or the quality of placing the needs and welfare of others before oneself. This selfless concern for the good of other people has been described as the golden rule of ethics. Altruism is motivation to do good for the sake of doing good, not for any kind of reward.

Since students who utilize bullying behaviors have a need to feel powerful and be in total control of others the concept of altruism is in direct conflict. While bullies gain satisfaction and reinforcement from inflicting discomfort and pain on others and have little empathy or warmth towards their targets, the R.I.S.E. system teaches altruism or kindness towards others. Obviously, altruism and bullying are incompatible behaviors. The literature recognizes that incompatible behaviors can be strengthened through the application of reinforcement. The R.I.S.E. system was designed with this principle in mind. If you are rewarded for being to class on time then that eliminates the possibility of being late. Therefore, if you have identified that a problem with students is that they are frequently late for class you can eliminate that behavior by rewarding them for being on time for class. This is often referred to as differential reinforcement of incompatible behavior. As we all know being kind to people is incompatible with bullying and the R.I.S.E. system reinforces behavior that often fall in the category of altruism. Thus we eliminate bullying type behaviors by rewarding altruistic behaviors. Further, since R.I.S.E. employs operant conditioning and is basically a reward based system students have less exposure to punishment based systems. Many bullies come from homes where physical punishment is used and children are taught to strike back physically as a way of dealing with problems. The R.I.S.E. program emphasizes reward and not punishment, therefore, once again it teaches a behavior incompatible with bullying. Although there is little evidence to support the contention that bullies victimize others because they feel bad about themselves (Batsche & Knoff, 1994) our experience shows youngsters with low self-esteem tend to become bullies.

Cyber bullying is bullying using electronic technology in-cluding devices and equipment such as cell phones, computers, and tablets, as well as, communication tools including social media sites, text messaging, chat rooms, and websites. Children who are cyber bullied are often bullied in person, as well.

According to STOPBULLYING.gov, cyber bullying is dif-ferent because "Cyber bullying can happen 24 hours a day, 7 days a week, and reach a kid even when he or she is alone. It can happen anytime of the day or night. Cyber bullying mes-sages and images can be posted anonymously and distributed quickly to a very wide audience. It can be difficult and some-times impossible to trace the source." The R.I.S.E. program has been helpful in reducing and even eliminating cyber bullying for the reasons stated above, namely teaching and rewarding al-truistic behavior and reinforcing behaviors incompatible with cyber bullying.

Further, because Maplebrook is a boarding school that espouses a very structured environment we have adopted some simple, but powerful guidelines for our faculty to follow. First, we attempt to be aware of what our students are doing online. We speak with them regarding their online activities and are able to monitor their use of websites. We "friend" our students on social media sites and we monitor the use of cell phones. Most importantly we reward appropriate use of electronic technology.

Our school has established rules about appropriate use of computers, cell phones, and other technology. For example, we are clear about what sites they can visit and what they are permitted to do when they are online. Parents and students sign an internet use policy that our faculty and staff monitor. We teach internet safety in our computer classes. We encourage all students to keep their passwords safe and not to share them with friends because sharing passwords can compromise their contact over their online identities and activities.

In the general school population students who have special needs can be targets especially with the current emphasis on mainstreaming. According to USL Legal Home mainstreaming is described as follows:

> "Pursuant to the Individuals with Disabilities Education Act (IDEA) all Americans with disabilities has the right to a free public education. Mainstreaming is the practice aimed at providing a positive educational experience for special education students. Through this special education students are placed in the regular education classroom for part of the school day. The aim of mainstreaming is to give special education students the opportunity to gain appropriate socialization skills

and access to the same education as regular education students while still allowing them access to resource rooms and special education classrooms.

Now-a-days mainstreaming has become a regular practice at many schools. Special educations students can be mainstreamed into a regular education classroom for part of the school day. Mainstreaming is customizable and often relies on the judgment of the regular classroom teacher and the special education teacher, both of whom will keep in constant communication to clearly evaluate a student's progress. Mainstreaming allows the special education student to take full advantage of all resources available to them."

As with many well intentioned laws, what is seen as a pure, fair and democratic action has turned into less than what was hoped by their supporters. Because special needs youngsters are "different" they frequently become easy targets of bullies. To understand this we should look closer into what makes many special needs students different. Some of them look different and that makes them susceptible to barbs and school yard taunts. Most of them are not good at understanding the subtleties of sarcasm and teasing. The nuances of language are frequently confusing to special needs students, therefore, potential bullies can say one thing, but in such a way that the special needs student does not realize the statement is mean and vicious. Special needs students are easy to persuade. Many are eager to please and wish to be part of the group, so they tend to do whatever other students tell them to do. Special needs students sometimes do not dress as well as other students and they may not be as conscious of cleanliness as other students. Many have poor eating habits and some have speech articulation issues. There are a multitude of other areas that cause special needs students to stand out as different to their peers and can give cause to them becoming a target for bullying.

Please be aware that there are many more nice students who treat special needs students with sensitivity and kindness, but it is that one bad apple that can make going to school extremely unpleasant.

One of the advantages of a school like Maplebrook is that although our students are all different they have a common bond: they all have a learning problem, and what is stressed at the school, through the R.I.S.E. program, is acceptance of individual differences. Further, since we are a boarding school and most of the faculty and staff live on campus, we are a close knit community.

21

R.I.S.E. at Home

Students' social and psychological welfare is important for academic success. Schools are responsible for teaching academics and also for promoting social growth of students, providing protective support to students, and supporting environments that allow students to cope with issues and problems. Learning pro-social behavior skills is one of the prime goals of the R.I.S.E. program. According to Amanda Lannie, Ph.D., "... it is true that a certain degree of anti-social behavior is considered normal. However, when children repeatedly engage in these anti-social acts, then there is cause for concern."

There are many different characteristics of children who exhibit anti-social behavior including aggressiveness, destructiveness, and deceitful behavior such as lying, breaking promises, and avoiding obligations. In more serious cases they are involved in stealing, shoplifting, and other behaviors which demonstrate a lack of respect for normal social conventions. Many children with these types of difficulties fail to comply with adult direction. They also fail to follow rules, openly defy parental restrictions, and repeatedly fail to meet expected responsibilities. Students who experience language based learning difficulties possess many of these same characteristics.

Over the years parents of Maplebrook students have reported their frustrations in dealing with their children who refuse to accept responsibility for their behaviors. With the outstanding success of the R.I.S.E. program over the last quarter century, many parents have asked if they can utilize some of its principles when their children are at home on vacations.

Several years ago we conducted a small R.I.S.E. at home program to explore if such a program would be a viable option to parents. To participate in the trial program parents were required to attend a workshop detailing the R.I.S.E. principles and procedures with the emphasis being on reinforcing the behaviors that parents wished to be increased and/or strengthened. Parents were also asked to keep in mind the four major teaching techniques outlined in the R.I.S.E. methodology:

1. *Insight Learning* – This method requires the recognition of cognitive processes that facilitate the acquisition of knowledge. Assuming the existence of a good helping relationship, students frequently profit from discussions leading to the understanding of why they feel and perform in a certain way. Although the discussion may not lead to immediate results, frequently the student will make a connection and arrive at an understanding of the situation later in life. I would like to illustrate this complex process by describing an experience I had as a youngster. As an eight-year-old growing up in an urban environment, one of my fondest activities was playing stickball. My family lived in a two-story house with a small, treed backyard. Being one of the few grass and treed areas in the neighborhood, our relatives arrived each Sunday afternoon for a day of relaxation and fun that culminated in an elaborate cookout. Part of the Sunday ritual was the division of individuals. The children

would flock to the street to play stickball, the mothers would busy themselves with conversation and preparation at the picnic table, and the fathers would retire to a shaded area near the fireplace to discuss local issues and engage in games of chance. One Sunday afternoon, I left the stickball game and returned to the picnic area to get a drink of water. As I approached the area where the water was kept, I observed my father was taking "dead aim" at a squirrel high in a tree. My father was armed with a hand-crafted slingshot loaded with a shiny marble. He launched his deadly missile with great accuracy, and the squirrel fell to the ground. I was absolutely devastated in observing my father kill this harmless creature. In tears, I chastised him for his cruelty. He looked at me, shaking his head in disagreement, and calmly explained that he couldn't kill the squirrel because he was using a round marble. His logic proceeded to explain that when a round marble hit the round head of the furry creature, it merely stunned him and he would soon recover. He had me help him gather some stones, place them in a circle behind the fireplace, and then he gently placed the unconscious animal in the center of the circle. He told me that if I waited for a few hours, the squirrel would recover and return to the trees. I was relieved, and after a short period of time returned to the stickball game. Several hours passed and the children were called in to supper. I ran to the circle of stones, and sure enough, the squirrel was gone. He had recovered just as my father had indicated.

Ten years later, I sat in my Army barracks in Texas recovering from a brief illness. I was rather lonely, having just turned eighteen and being two thousand miles from home. Then all of a sudden it struck me – my father had fooled me! The round marble, the circle of stone, the explanation, had been an elaborate scheme to reduce the grief of an eight-year-old. But somehow through an unknown cognitive process, ten years later an insight into the incident was gained.

At Maplebrook, the mentoring program allows teachers and students to discuss items of importance with each other on a weekly basis. This vehicle can be used to help students gain an understanding of their behavior and the behavior of others. Students and teachers have the opportunity to increase their understanding of a variety of current issues. This format builds upon a helping relationship and appropriate ego supports to foster growth in the student's ability to be responsible.

Frequently, in a counseling situation when discussing areas of responsibility, a student is unable to understand or accept the burden of responsibility. In spite of this, it should be emphasized, discussion is essential to the possible growth in understanding by the student. Perhaps a conversation between the student and teacher will yield results several months hence.

2. *Modeling* – One of the fundamental means of acquiring new behaviors and maintaining existing behaviors is through the use of modeling. Bandura (1969) indicates that "...virtually all learning phenomena resulting from direct experiences can occur on a vicarious basis through observation of other persons' behavior and its consequences for them." The key phrase to bear in mind is, "and its consequences for them." This stresses the notion that behavior is controlled or influenced by its consequences. It seems reasonable to assume that faculty will reinforce behavior that is appropriate, especially if faculty feel the student is performing a preferred response by imitating more appropriate peer models.

Browning and Stover (1971) indicate "...that the role of imitation is necessary in the acquisition of appropriate social behaviors in the residential center." Students learn by observing and "copying" the behaviors of "high status" students and faculty members. In fact, it should be constantly remembered that faculty and staff have a certain quality in the eye of the student. Students admire certain staff members and attempt to model their behaviors. A student who successfully "copies" a behavior of a "high status" student receives a potential windfall of social reinforcers from staff, other students, and most importantly, from himself.

3. *Reinforcement* – During the past fifty years, no learning technique has received more attention than reinforcement. In spite of its apparent simplicity and predictability, this technique is frequently used inappropriately by caring adults. In addition, many adults visualize the process of reinforcement to be no different than bribery. Let us examine that issue at this time. Bribery is the payment, given now, for a behavior or action to be accomplished at a future time. In addition, the term connotes something dishonest or unethical. Reinforcement is the "payment" given after the completion of a behavior or action. Thus, one difference is the temporal sequencing of the payment. The Bribe comes before the behavior and the Reward comes after the behavior. In fact, when you think about it, reinforcement is similar to our paycheck system. We generally get paid for work accomplished. Therefore, we may visualize the reinforcement process as being similar to the work ethic – you work hard to obtain rewards. This concept of positive reinforcement would take the form of Rrs↑, or a response (R) followed by a reinforcing stimulus (rs) increases (↑) the probability of that response occurring again.

Frequently, when discussing reward learning, there exists a confusion regarding the negative reinforcement and punishment. It should be noted that neither technique is able to teach and sustain behavior to the same degree as positive reinforcement. That is, learning that occurs through positive reinforcement develops faster and is sustained longer than learning obtained by the techniques of negative reinforcement or punishment.

The term negative reinforcement was originally developed to describe a series of events that appeared to be the converse of the application of a reward. In fact, the "reward" came when a noxious stimulus was removed. Thus, rather than the application of a reward to increase the frequency of a behavior, this concept of a negative reinforcement would take the form of R-as↑, or a response (R) followed by the removal of an aversive stimulus (-as) increases (↑) the probability of that response occurring again. It is called a reinforcer because it increases (↑) the probability of the response occurring again. It is part of a process that facilitates the acquisition of a behavior.

On the other hand, punishment is visualized as an inhibitor – something that suppresses an existing response. Punishment would be represented conceptually by the formula Ras↓, or a response (R) followed by the application of an aversive stimulus (as) decreases (↓) the probability of that response occurring again. It should be remembered that punishment is an effective learning technique when applied in a judicious manner. The major drawback when using punishment is the potential damage to the self-esteem of the individual being punished.

Positive reinforcement facilitates learning faster than any other learning technique and has the added benefit of strengthening the self-esteem of the individual being rewarded. Therefore, based on the principles of learning and the tenets of good mental health, positive reinforcement is the teaching technique of choice in a special education setting.

4. *Repetition* – Students frequently learn through the simple process of repetition. This process is based on the concept

that simply repeating a behavior time and time again will facilitate learning. The success of this method may be attested to by the legions of former students who have learned their multiplication tables using this time-honored method. For some students, this technique can be a reassuring method of learning, while other students may see this as a boring exercise that simply wastes time. In a boarding school setting, this technique relies strongly on structured activities occurring at a prearranged time and in a regular fashion. This reliance on structure and schedule can be comforting to students who lack confidence and self-discipline.

Parents were required to reward their child when they performed the target behavior. We supplied a customized "tally sheet" to be completed by the parent and returned to the R.I.S.E. Committee once the student returned to school. If the student performed well when they were at home they could earn a "free pass" or "save" card. This could be used during the year when they may have committed an infraction that may jeopardize their R.I.S.E. level. They could use the save pass to maintain their R.I.S.E. level and thus avoid a penalty. Another way to use the points accumulated while at home would be if a youngster was slightly below the necessary achievement level to advance to another R.I.S.E. level they could use the free pass card they earned while performing the R.I.S.E. at home program. The value added nature of the reinforcers became quite popular with students and many requested their parents participate in the R.I.S.E. at home program.

The program is designed to assist parents in providing structure during their child's everyday activities while they are at home. The structure would contain many elements familiar to their child. The program stresses the application of positive reinforcement when a child meets their responsibilities (as defined by the parent) while they are at home. At the same time the program is designed to reduce the amount an adult has to "keep after" the child until he/she complies with adult directives.

Needless to say all of us who are parents realize that parenting is not an easy task. In fact it may be the most difficult task an adult undertakes in his/her life. I have learned much as a parent, most of it is information not taught in schools and college. "Keeping after" a child until they comply with an adult request is often simply a euphemism for "nagging." Most of us were raised by caring parents who "kept after" us until we did what we were asked. In many cases these reminders crossed the line into nagging behavior.

Parents frequently tell their children that they are only demonstrating that they care for them. What is the difference between caring and nagging? This is a difficult question and reminds me when I was on a two and a half hour flight from New York City to Chicago. The moment I had sat down in my seat a woman asked me if I would change seats with her so she could sit next to her son. I agreed and she told me his seat number and went to him to bring him to his new seat. My new seat was two rows behind this woman and her son who appeared to be sixteen years old. As soon as she got him settled in, she started saying the following:

1. Put on your seat belt.

2. Put this blanket over your legs.

3. If you want to read, the switch for the light is up here.

4. If you want fresh air use this vent.

5. Once the stewardesses started circulating the cabin she immediately ordered water for the boy.

6. She then interrogated him as to what snack he preferred. Because he just shrugged and said he wasn't hungry she ordered something and told him he needed to keep his strength up. When it came he politely unwrapped it took one bite and the rest was discarded.

7. She then told him to sleep because the trip would seem shorter that way.

8. She then asked the stewardess for headphones so her son could listen to music.

I believe this vignette illustrates the differences between nagging and caring. Remember the son was sixteen and the mom was treating him like a toddler. One needs to respect emerging adults and give them space. I learned an important lesson when I witnessed this interaction: if we want our children to learn to take responsibility we should allow them to at least make decisions on the simple things. While each parent/child relationship is unique and special I believe if you keep nagging on small things a child will have difficulty learning independence and responsibility, further, they will grow to resent adult authority.

The R.I.S.E. at Home program stresses reward for compliance and reduces the number of "reminders" given. We need to give them space. I know a mother who will patiently wait outside the bathroom with a towel in her hand when her son took a shower. Why can't she train him to take one on his own? And all this when he was in college. I know a twenty year old girl who called her mother daily to obtain advice as to what to wear that day.

Parenting Style

The R.I.S.E. at Home program was designed to add a specific type of structure for a Maplebrook student while they are at home on vacation. That structure does impact on an individual's parenting style, but does not change it. You are simply asked to clearly define your expectations of your child and methodically recognize when they meet those expectations. In addition, the parent is only allowed to issue two reminders to the student; thus reducing the possibility of caring comments becoming nagging comments.

Twenty five years ago when I was Headmaster, a parent asked me to help her with her son when he was at home. I asked her to create a list of behaviors she would like to help him with. She indicated he was lazy and she wanted to help him with his lazy behavior. Later as she spoke we discovered he was also lazy because he did not do his chores and he did not keep his room clean and finally he did not do his homework. From this I learned that a large number of "undesirable" behaviors were not behaviors at all. They were merely labels applied to the absence of desirable behaviors. For example, when looking at what this mother was wanting to change in her child we discovered the mother wanted the son to clean his bedroom, do his chores, and do his homework. When he didn't do these things she applied the term "lazy" as a negative behavior for not accomplishing the tasks which were expected of him. Therefore, once we defined those behaviors incompatible with the described laziness we had specific behaviors we could strengthen and once the child starts to perform the desired behaviors, the undesirable behaviors automatically disappear.

As adults we have a tendency to "label" behaviors that are not behaviors at all. We might be better served to talk about behaviors that are either on-task or off-task. On-task behaviors are the expected behavior for a specific task e.g. being to class on time where off-task behavior is when the expected behavior is not achieved e.g. being late for class. This classification system is much more objective.

In sum, when parents are going to employ R.I.S.E. at Home techniques they should adhere to the following:

1. Define the behavior you wish to remove (off task).

2. Define the desired behavior (on task).

3. Reward the on task behavior.

4. "Reminders" should be limited to one or two.

5. Demonstrate your approach frequently.

6. Keep in mind the "principle of incompatibility."

7. Record the on task behavior on the score sheet.

8. Be sure your child brings the score sheet to the R.I.S.E. Committee when he/she returns to school.

Some final thoughts:

1. I would like to end this section by encouraging fathers to become involved in the R.I.S.E. at Home Program. Fredrick Buechner, son-in-law of one of Maplebrook's founders once wrote, "When a child is born, a father is born. A mother is born too of course, but at least for her it's a gradual process. Body and soul, she has nine months to get used to what's happening. She becomes what's happening. But for even the best prepared father,

it happens all at once. One the other side of a plate-glass window, a nurse is holding up something roughly the size of a loaf of bread for him to see for the first time."

2. "Raising kids is part joy and part guerilla warfare." -Ed Asner

3. "Parents are not quite interested in justice, they are interested in quiet." -Bill Cosby, Ed.D.

4. "Teenagers are people who act like babies if they are not treated like adults." -Mad Magazine

Appendix A

R.I.S.E. Forms

Responsibility – School   YES   NO

1. Prepared for School   ____   ____

Student Name: _____

Date: _____

Upon arriving for morning assembly, a faculty member checks the student for preparedness for school. This includes, but is not limited to: appropriate dress, I.D. card, and overall neatness.

Responsibility – Classroom   YES   NO

2. Prepared for Class   ____   ____

3. Class Effort   ____   ____

4. Class Interaction   ____   ____

Student Name: _____

Class Period: _____

Faculty: _____

Date: _____

For each academic class period, the teacher fills out this R.I.S.E. slip for every student that is not on Contract. In order for the student to earn all his/her points, he/she must come to class on time, with homework completed, and all the proper materials; give a sincere effort through participation, and interact appropriately with both the teacher and his/her classmates. This slip is usually filled out within the last five minutes of the class period.

Responsibility – Team Sports   **YES**   **NO**

5. Prepared for Sport   ____   ____

6. Effort at Sport   ____   ____

7. Interaction at Sport   ____   ____

Student Name: _____

R.I.S.E.: RESPONSIBILITY INCREASES SELF-ESTEEM

Coach: _____

Date: _____

For this particular R.I.S.E. slip, the coach of each team sport checks the student for arriving to practice in a timely fashion, bringing all required equipment, effort, and interaction with both teammates and the coaches.

Responsibility – Study Hall	YES	NO
8. Prepared for activity	____	____
9. Activity Effort	____	____
10. Activity Interaction	____	____

Student Name: _____

Activity Period: _____

Faculty/Staff: _____

Date: _____

In the evenings, after dinner, the students attend enrichment activities and study halls. With this slip, points are earned by arriving to the activity on time and with the appropriate materials. Points are also earned for effort and appropriate behavior and interaction with both fellow students and staff. The faculty/staff member fills out the slip within the last five minutes of the activity period.

Responsibility – Independence	YES	NO
11. Room Care	____	____
12. Chores	____	____
13. Visiting	____	____
14. Interaction	____	____
15. Language	____	____
16. Altruism	____	____

Student Name: _____

Activity Period: _____

Faculty/Staff: _____

Date: _____

This responsibility has recently changed from one point earned to six possible points. The reasoning behind the change is that the students spend a good deal of time in the dormitory and one point could not possibly cover all the activities in the dorm. The room care point entails maintaining a neat and clean bedroom. The chore point requires that the student complete his/her assigned task in the dorm. The visiting point is earned when the student exercises respect for the personal space of others in the dorm and adheres to the rules regarding lights out. Interaction is based on peer and staff interaction both in the morning and at night. The language point is earned when the student refrains from inappropriate language and voice tone. The altruism point pertains to the student behaving in a charitable manner toward fellow students and/or staff members. These points are filled out each evening and during the week, while the students are in the dormitories.

Responsibility – Job Performance

Advanced & Apprentice Performance Sheet

Name _____ Week Ending _____

For the academic students, R.I.S.E. points are achieved by satisfactorily performing their assigned job. The supervisor checks an S or U on the student time card, indicating whether the student's work performance included things such as being on time, completing all tasks, attitude, and effort. Furthermore, the supervisor initials the time card each day and the student signs the time card at the end of the work week, to be handed in for allowance pay. The mentor then receives the time card and issues the appropriate points.

R.I.S.E. Academic Students – Weekly Summary Sheet

Student Name _____

Mentor Name _____

APPENDIX A

Rise Levels: Beginner (Orientation, 2, 2+),Intermediate (3, 3.2, 3.3, 3.4), Advanced (4), Independent (Contract, Contract +)

(blank if RISE slip not received)

Responsibility	Date	S	M	T	W	TH	F	S	
1. Prepared for School			1	1	1	1	1		5
2. Class – Prepared			6	6	3	6	6	3	30
3. Class – Effort			6	6	3	6	6	3	30
4. Class – Interaction			6	6	3	6	6	3	30
5. Team Sports				3	3	3	3		12
6. Study Hall – Prepared		2	2	2	2				8
7. Study Hall – Effort		2	2	2	2				8
8. Study Hall – Interaction		2	2	2	2				8
Independence		5	5	5	5	5			25
Work Performance (job & time card)									
Social Skill (bonus points)									
		11	30	33	24	33	22	9	156

Topics discussed at meeting:
  A. Total Possible Points
  B. Minus ___ P oints Not Earned
  C. Equals Points Earned

Recommendations: C / A = %
Each week, each faculty member must fill out a student weekly summary sheet on each mentee who is on one of the following R.I.S.E. levels; orientation, 2, 2+, 3, 3_2, 3_3, 3_4, or 4. This form allows the mentor to tally up the number of yes

and no points received from all the R.I.S.E. slips throughout the week in order to compute a total percentage of earned points. Furthermore, this form allows the mentor to comment on specific topics that were discussed during the weekly mentor/mentee meeting. After the percentage is computed, the mentor makes a recommendation as to whether the student should move up a R.I.S.E. level, remain at the present level, or drop a level.

R.I.S.E. Program Contract – Independent Level #4

Student Name _____

Date: _____

Responsibilities:
1. I will be prepared for school and activities each day.
2. I will be responsible for trying my best to learn in school.
3. I will be responsible for interacting appropriately with staff and students.
4. I will be responsible for my room and clothing care, dorm chores, and personal hygiene.
5. I will follow all Maplebrook School rules.
6. I will participate in the Maplebrook Leadership Training Program.

APPENDIX A

Privileges:

1. I will be eligible to spend free time in the Student Center or computer lab when open.

2. I will be eligible for off-campus activities and unaccompanied by staff.

3. I will be eligible to order take-out food from local restaurants.

4. I will be eligible to participate in "dress-down" days.

5. I will be eligible to be a member of the Society of Honor.

6. I will be eligible to use dormitory Contract Room.

7. I will be eligible to eat lunch at picnic tables.

8. I will be eligible to plan special weekend activities through Leadership Group

I understand that if I follow this contract, I can remain on the Independent Level.

_____   _____

Student's Signature   Date

_____   _____

Mentor's Signature   Date

_____   _____

Faculty with Dormitory   Date
Responsibilities Signature

_____   _____

R.I.S.E. Committee Signature   Date

_____   _____

Headmaster's Signature   Date

Independent Level #4: Contract

Once a student has earned his/her way to R.I.S.E. Level 4, he/she may begin to fill out a Contract. The contract is indicative of the student's ability to act responsibly, and as a result, more privileges are available to him/her. The contract outlines specific responsibilities that the student must adhere to, as well as eight given privileges for the student. As an extra bonus the student may choose three of his/her own privileges that may include, but are not limited to: study hall in the dorm, more off-campus weekend trips, or visiting friends in another dormitory. Once the extra privileges are checked by the mentor, the student and mentor sign the contract, and it is dated. It is then sent to the faculty member who has dormitory responsibilities where the student is housed, and turned into the R.I.S.E. committee for approval. Once all of the appropriate signatures are achieved, the student's contract is sent to the Headmaster for final review and signature.

R.I.S.E. Contract Students

Weekly Summary Report

Student Name _____

Date _____

Mentor's Name _____

TOPICS OF DISCUSSION

A. <u>Relationship with Peers: (Events, Concerns, etc.)</u>

B. <u>Interactions with Teachers, F.D.R.'s, etc.</u>

C. <u>Activities, Classroom Learning Experiences, Work Assignments:</u>

Mentor's observations/recommendations:

R.I.S.E. Weekly Summary for Contract Students

At the end of each week, mentors who have students on contract or contract plus must fill out a weekly summary sheet. This sheet outlines the specific areas that are addressed during the mentoring session. The topics of discussion include, but are not limited to: relationships with peers, interactions with teachers, faculty in the dormitories, coaches, and other staff, and any special activities or work assignments both in and out of the classroom. The final portion of this form allows the mentor to make any recommendations or voice concerns that he/she feels would be in the best interest of the student.

Mentor Update Meeting Format

Student Name _____

Date _____

Mentor's Name _____

Mentor Summary (including parent contact):

Academic (Career) Progress:

Residential Progress:

Peer Relationships:

Program Involvement:

Attitude and Motivation:

Medical Issues:

Clinical Reports:

R.I.S.E. Status:

Suggestions/Recommendations:

Student in Crisis: Concerns/Suggestions/Recommendations:

Mentor Update Meeting Format

The purpose of this form is to ensure that the mentor is aware of all aspects of the student's progress. Because the student comes in contact with several faculty and staff, it would be very difficult to have private meetings with everyone. Thus, upon request of any faculty member, a mentor update meeting is held in which all faculty and staff who have a specific exposure to the student attend and give feedback concerning the student. This form covers several areas that may need attention, specifically academic progress, residential concerns, and social progress including peer relationships, attitude, and motivation. This form is filed in the student's personal file for future reference.

Mentor Communication Log with Parents

Advisee: _____

Advisor: _____

Spoke to: _____

Date: _____

Summary of conversation:

Recommendations from parent/mentor:

Monthly Mentor Communication Log with Parents

Twice each month, the mentor places a telephone call to the parents of his/her mentee in order to brief the parents or guardian on the student's progress. This form indicates the mentee's name, mentor's name, to whom the mentor spoke, and the date of the telephone call. Throughout the conversation, the mentor writes notes about topics covered with the parent or guardian regarding his/her student. If there are any specific recommendations or suggestions from the parent or guardian, it is indicated on the bottom of the form. The purpose of this form is not only to keep the parent or guardian current on the student's progress, but to enable the mentor to stay focused on the student's past accomplishments and future goals, with input from the parents or guardian.

Bibliography

Adelman, H.S., & Taylor, L. *Intrinsic Motivation and School Misbehavior: Some Intervention Implications.* Journal of Learning Disabilities, Vol. 23, 541, 550, 1990.

Banks, Ron. *Bullying in Schools.* ERIC, 1997.

Brilhart, J.K. *Effective Group Discussion.* Dubuque: Brown Publishers. 1986.

California Task Force to Promote Self Esteem *Toward A State of Self Esteem.* California State Department of Education. 1990.

Coopersmith, S. *The Antecedents of Self Esteem.* San Francisco: Freeman & Co. 1967.

Fazzone, R.A. *The Child Care Professional: Looking Forward.* Elmsford: Collegium Press. 1981.

Fazzone, R.A. *Sabbatical Report.* Poughkeepsie: Dutchess Community College. 1980.

Fazzone, R.A. *Working With Troubled Children and Youth.* Elmsford: Collegiate Press. 1979.

Geiser, R. *The Illusion of Caring.* Boston: Beacon Press. 1973.

Haber, Joel *Bullyproof Your Child for Life.* New York: Penguin Books. 2007

Knoff, H.M. & Batsche, G.M. Project Archive. School Psychology Review, 24 (4), 579-603. 1995.

Lannie, Amanda. *Increasing the Effectiveness of Self Monitoring Programs.* Dissertation. Syracuse University. 2006

Lickona, T. *Education for Character.* New York: Bantam Books. 1991.

Rogers, C.R. *Counseling and Psychotherapy.* Boston: Houghton. 1942.

Scully, J.L. *The Power of Social Skills in Character Development: Helping Diverse Learners Succeed.* New York: Dade Publishing. 2000.

Spafford, C.S. & Grosser, G.S. *The Social Misperception Syndrome in Children with Learning Disabilities: Social Causes Versus Neurological Variables.* Journal of Learning Disabilities, 189, 1993.

Trieschman, A., Whittaker, J., and Brendtro, L. *The Other 23 Hours.* Chicago: Aldine Publishing. 1969.

www.ingramcontent.com/pod-product-compliance
Lightning Source LLC
Chambersburg PA
CBHW051412280526
45785CB00003B/1043